the Shopping Bags

the Shopping Bags

Tips, Tricks, and

Inside Information

to Make You a Savvy Shopper

Anna Wallner
& Kristina Matisic

NEW AMERICAN LIBRARY

New American Library
Published by New American Library, a division of Penguin Group (USA) Inc., 375 Hudson Street, New York, New York 10014, USA • Penguin Group (Canada), 90 Eglinton Avenue East, Suite 700, Toronto, Ontario M4P 2Y3, Canada (a division of Pearson Penguin Canada Inc.) • Penguin Books Ltd., 80 Strand, London WC2R 0RL, England • Penguin Ireland, 25 St. Stephen's Green, Dublin 2, Ireland (a division of Penguin Books Ltd.) • Penguin Group (Australia), 250 Camberwell Road, Camberwell, Victoria 3124, Australia (a division of Pearson Australia Group Pty. Ltd.) • Penguin Books India Pvt. Ltd., 11 Community Centre, Panchsheel Park, New Delhi - 110 017, India • Penguin Group (NZ), cnr Airborne and Rosedale Roads, Albany, Auckland 1310, New Zealand (a division of Pearson New Zealand Ltd.) • Penguin Books (South Africa) (Pty.) Ltd., 24 Sturdee Avenue, Rosebank, Johannesburg 2196, South Africa

Penguin Books Ltd., Registered Offices: 80 Strand, London WC2R 0RL, England

Published by New American Library, a division of Penguin Group (USA) Inc. Previously published in a Dutton edition.

First New American Library Printing, August 2006
10 9 8 7 6 5 4 3 2 1

Copyright © Anna Wallner and Kristina Matisic, 2005
All rights reserved

REGISTERED TRADEMARK—MARCA REGISTRADA

New American Library Trade Paperback ISBN: 0-451-21858-2

The Library of Congress has cataloged the hardcover edition of this title as follows:

Wallner, Anna.
   The shopping bags: tips, tricks, and inside information to make you a
savvy shopper/Anna Wallner and Kristina Matisic.
      p. cm.
   Includes bibliographical references and index.
   ISBN 0-525-94887-2
   1. Shopping.   I. Matisic, Kristina.   II. Title.
   TX335.W24 2005
   640'.73—dc22   2005008292

Set in Berkeley Medium • Designed by Daniel Lagin

Printed in the United States of America

The Shopping Bags television show is produced by the Shopping Bags Media Inc., a partnership between New Shoes Productions and Force Four Entertainment. It airs on the Fine Living Network and the W Network.

To my mother, who shares my love of shopping; and my father, who shares my love of books

—Kristina Matisic

For Blair   **—Anna Wallner**

Contents

Introduction

Have you ever had buyer's remorse? Surrendered to an impulse purchase at the mall? Did you shell out big bucks for that antiwrinkle cream only to find your wrinkles stayed put? And remember that pair of designer jeans that stretched all out of shape? (C'mon, 'fess up.) Do you always reach for the same brand-name glass cleaner even though the generic brand is half the price? (And is the glass in your home really so much cleaner as a result?) Don't even get us started on the grocery store, where brilliantly veiled marketing tricks have you at the checkout counter with a cartful of food when all you came in for was a loaf of bread. And what about that video camera you bought just last year? Do you really need the "optical image stabilizer"? (Actually, that is a good thing to have.) Or do you simply wonder if you can get that car, that sofa, the shoes, or the lightbulbs for less?

We can relate. The retail world is complicated—there are too many options, too much fine print, too many marketing ploys. If you're going to survive out there, you need to study up. You need a shopping encyclopedia. We are The Shopping Bags, and it's our mission to provide you with that reference and to make shopping easier for you.

WHO WE ARE

Several years ago we were just like you: We hated buying a T-shirt only to have it fall apart in the wash. A bad warranty meant we were stuck with a blender that conked out after three milk shakes. Fed up with wasted money and wasted time, we decided to do something drastic. We set out to research everything before we bought it—and never get ripped off again.

We started calling professionals from every walk of life—aestheticians, race car drivers, doctors, dentists, gardeners, even dog walkers—to ask questions about the products we buy. After all, who better to tell you which brand of garbage bag is best than a garbage man? And then we started testing the products ourselves—from lip gloss to lawn furniture to luggage. Soon we had a stockpile of information, things that other shoppers might just want to know about.

> Ten o'clock on weekday mornings is the best time to shop—especially if you're making a return—as crowds are low.

Many afternoons of shoe shopping and brainstorming later, we came up with the concept for *The Shopping Bags*. We quit our day jobs as journalists at a local TV station and committed ourselves to researching consumer products and providing shoppers with tips, tricks, and inside information on everything they buy. For the past five years, the results of our findings have been airing on our hit TV show. Then it was time to put pen to paper and give you a fun, fact-filled shopping guide you can carry with you to the store.

Today's shopper is hungry for the information we offer. Yes, we all want to make the right shopping choice—but no, we don't all want to spend two months researching the matter. (After all, it's only a lightbulb!) With this book, you'll gain the upper hand. You can look up products before you buy them, and see where the pitfalls are. You can have the results of our tests and research right at your fingertips.

As far as we're concerned, shopping is not just a way to get the stuff you need and want; it's also a sport. And we play to win!

WHAT WE DO AND HOW WE DO IT

Basically, we do your homework for you. It's a rigorous five-step process:

Step one involves analyzing the information—*all* the information—on each and every product we cover. Books, articles, lab reports, research data, instructional booklets, and advertising material—you name it, we sift through it.

Step two involves picking up the phone and dialing up the world's most reputable and well-known experts. We've interviewed fashionistas like Diane von Furstenberg and Lars Nilsson, domestic divas like Martha Stewart, Olympic athletes like Picabo Street, and some of the best-known personalities in the world of cars, gardens, and beauty.

But we go way beyond the bigwigs and celebrities. **Step three** involves hitting the front lines and grilling the people who use and abuse the products we're investigating. We talk to dog walkers about the personalities of different breeds; we chat with garbage men about which bags really make it to the curb; we question day-care workers about the safest and most user-friendly high chairs; and we spy on hairdressers to see what kinds of hair products they use on themselves.

Step four involves personally testing every product and taking our tests to the extreme. We ride roller coasters to test hair spray, rock-climb to test nail polish, and who can forget the time Anna put the condom over her head to prove that a regular-size rubber can fit most men! Products take over every available closet, counter, and square inch of flooring in our homes. At any one time, we're testing half a dozen different things: exercise gizmos litter the living room; blush, hair mousse, and face moisturizers battle each other for space on the bathroom counter; and jars of peanut butter, cans of tomato sauce, and boxes of frozen pizza squeeze out anything resembling real food in the fridge. It's safe to say we take a hands-on approach to our business. We want to know how each and every product stands up to—well—us! And we want to pass that information on to you.

But we're not done there. **Step five** involves making sure each product and service suits each person's individual needs and styles. Deciding on the right product depends on your requirements, your desires, and your budget. We arm you with the questions you need to ask and the things you need to look for to determine which makes and models are right for you.

THE TEN SHOPPING COMMANDMENTS

Having logged many hours at the stores, we've learned a few simple truths. We call them the Ten Shopping Commandments—ten rules we apply to each and every shopping experience. These guidelines help us get what we want, get it for less, and be more informed about the stuff we buy.

1. NEGOTIATE!

Not on sale? Ask for a discount anyway. It doesn't mean you're cheap; it means you understand competition and that retailers are all fighting for your shopping dollar. And remember, bargaining is a way of life in many cities around the globe. Here are some tips for bargaining made easy:

Don't ask for a specific amount, like 10 percent off the price tag, for example. You never know when you're leaving money on the table. Instead, simply say, "Can you give me a better deal?" This gambit also leaves room for the retailer to throw in something extra in lieu of cutting the price. (That is how Kristina got free delivery with her new mattress.)

Give the store a reason to discount. Buying flowers for a dinner party that night? Blooms slightly past their prime will probably do you just fine, and you've got a reason for a discount. Dented can of tuna? Ha!

Take a friend. Many people find bargaining nerve-racking, at least in the beginning. So take a friend along for moral support the first couple of times. Your pal can also pipe in if you're ever at a loss for words.

Be nice. If a salesperson likes you, he or she is more likely to want to give you a discount. (See Commandment #6.)

Be prepared to walk away. Chances are you may be able to nab a better price elsewhere. When a salesman wouldn't give Anna any discount on a two-thousand-dollar computer, she went straight to the manufacturer's store and got it for three hundred dollars less.

You won't succeed in getting a better deal every time, but it never hurts to ask. And once you start saving money and getting free stuff regularly, negotiating will become a habit.

2. MAKE A DATE

Every line of merchandise has an end of season, so get your calendar and jot down our version of an almanac:

January to March: Activewear. New merchandise tends to come in between January and March, so that's the perfect time to get a good deal on last year's styles. Winter clothes also hit the sales rack at this time of year.

May to September: Paint. While some manufacturers put their interior paints and deck stains on sale in time for spring cleaning, the biggest sales and deepest discounts on interior and exterior paints happen on long weekends in the summer—specifically, Memorial Day, Fourth of July, and Labor Day weekends.

June: Running shoes. Manufacturers are under the gun to come up with new running-shoe models every six months—so look for sales in the winter, too.

July and August: Clothing sales. Like clockwork, clothes start going on sale the first weekend of July, leaving you lots of summertime left to enjoy your new, low-priced duds.

Winter: Used vehicles generally show their worst characteristics during the winter months, so dealers and private sellers are less hard-nosed about sticking to the list price.

Of course, not every sale corresponds to a particular time of year. Keep a watchful eye on big chain stores. Lots of stock and high turnover mean there will always be sale items available. (Read: Never pay full price for towels or a mattress!)

Before ordering something online, read the site's privacy policy. It tells you what personal information the Web site operators are collecting and how this information will be used. If you can't find one, take your business elsewhere (or be prepared for them to use your information however they wish).

And finally, know the delivery schedules at your favorite stores—especially big-box stores and plant nurseries. You'll get the most sizes to choose from, the freshest flowers and plants, and the best selection overall. Having the "pick of the litter" means you can buy knowing you didn't miss out on something better.

3. KNOW WHAT YOU NEED

We all want quality. But defining what quality means to each of us has a lot to do with our wants, our needs, our lifestyles, and our pocketbooks. Every toaster will make toast. But how many settings you require and how many you are willing to pay for depends on you. (Do you really need that bagel button?) When matching your requirements to the right product, there are a few things to consider:

Brands. Brand names often do cost more but that isn't always a bad thing. Big manufacturers often have solid reputations and can be more than willing to stand behind their products should something go wrong. Paying for peace of mind can be worth it.

Features. What makes the price of one TV $575, when a similar model costs $750? Added features can double or even triple the price. The trick here is deciding among the features you need, the features you want, and the features you can afford. Take the personal digital assistant, for example. After thinking about how she'd really use it, Kristina turned away from the fancy PDA with the full-color screen and settled on a more basic monochromatic model that cost a hundred dollars less.

Materials and workmanship. The materials used in manufacturing also play a big role in the final price. A lightweight Kevlar kayak *is* super easy to maneuver through rushing water, but seriously, will that placid country lake you'll be using it on ever rock your boat?

Realistically analyzing what is worth paying for is key to helping you strike a balance between what you yearn for and what your pocketbook can handle.

4. DON'T BE A SUCKER

Time and time again, our tests have shown that there are some types of products that just aren't worth paying more for. If you know what to look for on the label, you can get great alternatives at lower prices for many everyday items.

Antiaging products. Unless you're buying directly from your dermatologist, the antiwrinkle cream in the pretty box may not be any more effective than the stuff at the drugstore. And keep in mind that over-the-counter antiaging products often don't contain high enough concentrations of the active ingredient, be it vitamin C or retinol. For specific ingredient guidelines, look up antiaging products (including cellulite treatments, facial moisturizers, and wrinkle cream) in the encyclopedia section of this book.

Cleaning products. Generic or store-brand window cleaners, all-purpose cleaners, and toilet bowl cleaners all work just as well as brand names. (And vinegar is a great substitute for both glass cleaner and antibacterial products.)

Makeup. Two huge corporations—Estée Lauder and L'Oréal—own the vast majority of cosmetics lines. For example, Estée Lauder's lineup includes Aveda, Bobbi Brown, Clinique, MAC, Origins, and the chichi La Mer! This means that the low-end and the high-end lipsticks may very well come from the same factory. Getting the right shade and texture is the more important consideration, and there are great products at both the drugstore and the department store. When shopping at the drugstore, ask to have packages opened so you can test colors and consistency.

Shampoo and conditioner. No silver bullet here—the active ingredients are essentially the same for all products. The main difference lies in the concentration of the conditioning ingredients (such as panthenol, collagen, and elastin). Again, you can find good products at both the salon and the drugstore. Anna swears by drugstore brands for day to day, but then prefers using salon brands about once a week for deep conditioning and cleaning.

Like fancy packaging or the latest and greatest designers? Believe us, we understand why you do. It's okay to buy expensive things as long as you know *why* you're spending the big bucks. And if you know what you're paying for, you'll never feel like you've been had.

5. BE A SMARTY-PANTS

When it comes to making those really big purchases, you may have to put in a little extra time. Remember, homework means money in your pocket. Follow these simple guidelines, and you'll wind up knowing more than the average salesperson.

Start here. This book will provide the top things you should consider when making a particular purchase, if we do say so ourselves.

Hit the Web. But tread carefully, shopping sisters! While the Internet can be a gem, some sites are, let's just say, less than accurate. We like to see a fact supported by at least two sources before we believe it. We recommend visiting consumer opinion Web sites where you can find out how others reviewed a certain product. Kristina, for example, never books a hotel without first investigating what others thought of it. Read between the lines, take individual biases into account, and you can uncover a few nuggets of truth.

Don't be shy. Talk to friends and family about what products work for them. And go straight to the experts, as well. Talk to your doctor about health products and to repair people about appliances, and ask them which professional organizations to contact for more information. Your local Better Business Bureau also has the goods on reputable businesses in your area.

Phone ahead. When you've decided on a particular product, let your fingers do the shopping, and do some cost comparisons over the phone. Before you start driving all over town in search of that stereo, call to make sure the store has the product in stock. Think of all the money you'll save on gas and parking!

6. BE NICE

It's a simple rule, but one that can make or break your success at the store: Be nice to salespeople. We expect them to be courteous, efficient, knowledgeable, *and* to give us a deal. You're more likely to get what you want if you're friendly. This rule also applies to restaurants. Want a place where everybody knows your name? Tip early and tip well!

When service is good, we give

- 15 percent in restaurants and for beauty services
- 10 percent to the food delivery guy when he brings around pizza
- Fifty cents to three dollars for a taxi ride, depending on the distance and whether the cabbie carried your bags and held the door (some cab companies automatically charge extra for bags, so don't make the mistake of paying twice for this)
- One or two dollars to the bellhop for bringing up your bags
- One or two dollars a night to the maid at the hotel
- Twenty dollars to the concierge who has nabbed theater tickets or a coveted reservation (more if he or she has helped you out over several days)
- Twenty dollars to the paper delivery person at Christmas

But as always, read the fine print, especially in restaurants and hotels. Sometimes gratuity is included—especially in foreign countries. And when it comes to room service, gratuity and delivery charges are often added to the already astronomical food prices. (Makes us want to go hungry instead!)

Showing your gratitude is also about those little extras (remembering a birthday, a tip at Christmas, and so forth) that make your hairdresser, cleaning lady, or paperboy go the distance. They are working for you, after all, and no one wants to be thought of as a bad boss.

7. KICK THE TIRES

Before you take home any new product, always give it the once-over to make sure all the parts are in place, that there's no damage, and that the entire item is in good working order.

We all know this. But we also believe in taking items—especially big-ticket items—for a test drive.

No one in her right mind would buy a car without taking it out for a spin, right? That includes calling in a mechanic to look under the hood, and giving the vehicle a very careful examination. (And with a used car, it means checking all the panels, as slightly mismatched paint is often a sign of repairs after an accident.) We apply this same thinking to other purchases. When shopping for furniture, ask if you can take the piece out on loan to see if it fits your space and your tastes. If the retailer won't make these allowances, take your business elsewhere.

> Got a sweetie who hates shopping? When you need to make a big purchase, do all your browsing on your own. Narrow your choices down to a few before taking your other half with you to the mall.

With sporting goods, most stores will allow you to demo the tennis racket or the skis before you make the purchase. Again, if they won't accommodate you, move on. Expect to pay a small "demo" or rental fee. If you later decide to purchase that product, the demo fee should be deducted from the purchase price. Get a blister while jogging in those new runners? Take them back. Sporting goods is one area where we find merchants do a good job of standing behind their products.

If we're not satisfied, we'll return pretty much anything. We've returned jeans that didn't stretch as much as the salesperson promised, clothing that didn't wash well, and even beauty products that don't live up to their promises. (Anna's self-tanner wasn't producing a tan!)

8. STAY ON YOUR GAME

A salesperson's job is to sell. When you go to a store for a new snowboard, salespeople will also try to sell you the boots, socks, and perhaps some goggles. Up-selling and impulse buying can happen to the best of us.

We have a little trick that helps us stay on track. Before you go shopping, commit your budget and your requirements to a piece of paper, and put the note in your pocket. If you're feeling pressure to overspend or the desire to give in to temptation, pull out that paper as a reminder. When those numbers stare at you in black-and-white, they have a sobering effect. If you are still feeling pressured, experiencing information overload, or simply are not sure about a purchase, take a break, have a coffee, and clear your head. Time and distance can help you determine if you really want to buy.

Of course, there are times when it really is in your best interest to walk away, especially if you suspect that shady business practices are being used. For example, you see an ad in the paper hawking DVD players for fifty dollars. When you arrive at the store, you're told they sold out hours ago . . . but there's an even better DVD player in stock, for just twenty-five dollars more. That situation can be a sign of the old "bait and switch," whereby enticing ads are used to lure customers into a store to sell them a more expensive item than the one advertised. Advertising goods on sale with no intention of having enough in stock is a federal offense.

We also advise walking away from extended warranties. Profit margins on them can soar between 70 and 100 percent! And salespeople will take home about 35 to 50 percent of that profit. Only a very small percentage of electronics actually break down before the warranty expires. And repairs can often cost less than the warranty itself. With the notable exception of laptop computers (see page 116), we say take your chances without an extended warranty.

 9. KEEP YOUR COOL

Nothing ruins a fun-filled day of shopping like bad service. Like the time we went for dinner at a new hot spot, and the carpaccio was delivered without the olive oil and cheese that the menu had promised. Rather than remove the dish and get the kitchen to fix it, our waitress delivered a block of cheese and a side of oil to the table. If we'd wanted to make our own food, we would have stayed home!

The best way to complain is **in person**. It's much harder for an establishment to ignore a customer who's staring right at them. Our second choice is **a letter**, since it creates a paper trail. And regardless of the outcome, writing can be therapeutic. Complaining **by phone** is not our favorite method. Phones often mean being on hold and getting increasingly frustrated. And voice messages, especially complaints, have a way of not being returned. It's so easy to press that delete button. But many larger companies do have customer complaint lines where representatives will listen to your gripes. In these cases, we recommend using the service as a starting point. When making a consumer complaint, here are a few other tips to keep in mind:

Stay calm. We know you have a fabulous list of expletives you're just dying to blurt out—we've been there. The key to effective complaining is to show respect and to communicate effectively. And if you can, start your complaint with a compliment. You want to win this person over.

Be clear about what you want. Do you want a refund? A replacement? An apology? The only way to get what you want in life is to ask for it.

Talk to the right person. You'd like a manager, preferably. If the clerk wants to try to help first, let him. If you're complaining by letter or e-mail, phone ahead, get the name and title of the manager or head of customer service, and address your correspondence to that person specifically.

Be prompt. Retailers and service providers are much more likely to respond to your complaint if it's made immediately (provided you can keep your cool) or within a few days of the incident. A prompt reaction to the alleged shopping crime shows you are serious about getting the issue resolved. You're also more likely to remember all the details if you act right away.

Small or petite physique? Head to the juniors department when shopping for clothes. The duds there are cheaper, and it's a great place to search for basics such as T-shirts and the like.

If your efforts to settle a dispute go unheard or if you're unsatisfied with the response you get, your next step should be to contact your local Better Business Bureau. If the business or service belongs to a professional association, you can also lodge a complaint through that group.

Like negotiating, lodging a complaint is an empowering part of the shopping experience. Remember that retail is an increasingly competitive business. If you don't get what you want at one establishment, chances are good you'll get it somewhere else. And regardless of whether your complaint is well received, the whole exercise of communicating your concerns will leave you feeling more satisfied.

10. WEAR COMFORTABLE CLOTHES

Serious shoppers do not hit the stores wearing heels and a miniskirt. (Unless you're shopping for a man, we suppose.) For a day of pounding the pavement, you'll need to wear flat shoes and layers and carry a bag large enough to tote your lightweight jacket and your purchases. Also bring along water and snacks. Treat shopping like an endurance sport: You need proper sustenance and the right gear if you're going to go the distance. Perhaps this is an excuse to go shopping for flat shoes and a shopping bag!

Attention, Shoppers

Now it's time to check your shopping list. Are you in the market for a new party dress? Need some running shoes, red wine, a kayak, dish detergent, a baby crib, or a blender? The following pages contain the top tips to help you get the most for your money. Smart shopping doesn't always mean buying the cheapest item, and we all know by now that it doesn't mean buying the most expensive product either. Spotting quality begins with educating yourself. So read up before you hit the store, or take this guide along on your shopping expeditions. The alphabetical entries in each category make it easy to find the products you're shopping for and flip to the relevant page.

1. Dressed to the Nines: Fashion and Accessories

I t's a good time to be a clotheshorse. The market is saturated, making it easier than ever to find stylish clothes and designer knockoffs. To keep your closet au courant and your wallet intact, heed this advice and remember: At some time or another, just about *everything* goes on sale.

Avoid paying retail. This is especially true if you shop at chain stores like Banana Republic or department stores like Nordstrom, where eventually most merchandise goes on sale. Believe us, we've tested this theory! At the start of every season, we hit all the chain stores and make a list or take digital pictures of items we want, and then we track them. Whether you can wait for the sale price or if they'll still have your size in stock are the main considerations for paying full price or waiting it out. But don't forget to try Commandment #1: Negotiate!

Hit the discount stores. You *can* shop at places like Wal-Mart and still be stylish. Blend discount items with other designer pieces (like a bargain camisole with your favorite designer suit). Discount and off-price stores mark down designer clothing by about 30 percent to start with and go on from there. The best merchandise moves quickly though—these places are a hub for smart shoppers, so you'll definitely want to find out when new shipments arrive. Befriend the salesclerks!

Get on the sample sale circuit. Sample sales are a great way to get designer items for less. (These are garments and accessories that have been used to showcase a designer's new line.) Local retailers and designers offer low, low prices on a selection of sample sizes—which tend to be on the small side. To get onto the sample sale circuit, inquire with any independently owned clothing store or a local designer. Once you get on one list, you'll find you quickly get invited to lots of private sales. Much like designer warehouses, the best buys at these events get snapped up very quickly. Arrive promptly on the first day, but not too early; most sample sellers have a strict "no early birds" policy.

Find out whether your favorite stores offer sale adjustments. That means if you pay full price for something that goes on sale a week later, you get a refund or credit for the discounted amount.

Browse the Web. Online shopping is a great way to nab hard-to-find and vintage items (especially handbags). The eBay auction site is a good place to start hunting. But before buying, check the ratings of individual sellers, learn how to spot a fake (see below), and keep in mind that most bidding happens in the final minutes of an auction.

We like to check online stores to compare prices and watch for sales. And of course, we recommend shopping from sites that allow you to return the merchandise if it doesn't fit properly, as buying clothes sight unseen can be tricky unless you're familiar with the line. And don't forget to budget for shipping, handling, and currency conversion (if buying from outside the country).

Spot the real McCoy. Can you tell the difference between a Kate Spade and a Kate Splade? The problem with shopping at discount shops, secondhand stores, and online is that you're oftentimes weeding through lots of fakes. A fake is something that is designed to copy a designer brand; whereas a knockoff is designed to merely look similar. Of course, if you're not a purist, a knockoff is a great way to save money and stay stylish. But producing *fake* merchandise is an infringement of copyright laws and is therefore illegal. Buying the stuff is not illegal but remember, you are supporting criminal activity.

Whether it's a fake or a knockoff, here's what to look for:

- Labels. Are they sewn or glued on? Glued labels are a sure sign it isn't the real deal.
- Logos. Examine them closely. Is the name of the brand spelled correctly? Sometimes a knockoff will be slightly different (that is, *Carter* instead of *Cartier*).
- Lining. A true designer handbag is lined, often with leather.

Accessorize. A new pair of earrings, belt, or scarf can be a great way to update your wardrobe for just a few dollars. Accessories are one easy area to go cheap and still look like a million bucks. The key is to buy *simple* pieces, with few details.

Remember our seven-day rule and curb impulse buying. If you see something you just have to have—but don't really need—walk away. If it's still on your mind a week later, you were meant to be together.

There is so much selection out there today at so many price points, you can literally buy a pair of jeans for twenty-five dollars and a pair for five hundred dollars. So when should you spend more, and when should you spend less? We think it's worth investing in a business suit in a neutral color, boots, a winter coat made of wool (for those who live in colder climates); jeans that make you look and feel like a million bucks, and one basic handbag for daytime. We've found that if you hunt around, you can find quality T-shirts, sweaters, undergarments, and fun eveningwear without breaking the bank.

Whether you're looking to fill your drawers with basics like socks, undergarments, and tees; dressing to impress in a power suit and killer heels; or wandering the bridal boutiques to wow at your wedding, we've got you covered—head to toe.

The following is a list of commonly purchased clothing items and accessories, organized alphabetically so you can easily find what you're looking for. We've talked to the textiles experts, quizzed the designers, and personally tested every item listed below (except for the men's underwear—we admit we didn't wear those!) to ensure that you get the best value for your fashion dollar.

HERE'S WHAT'S IN OUR SHOPPING BAG

BRAS

- About 70 percent of women wear the wrong-size bra. We recommend shopping at specialty stores where staff can help you with a custom fit. (We both went up a cup size when we did this!)
- To determine your own fit, measure the distance directly under your breasts, all the way around your back. (Round up or down to the nearest even number, whichever is more comfortable for you.) Then measure from the fullest part of your breast (without a bra) all the way around (round up to the nearest even number). The difference between the two numbers will determine your cup size. Zero to 1½ inches difference means you're an A, 1½ to 2½ inches is a B, 2½ to 3½ indicates a C, and so on. But remember, this is only a starting point—not all 34Bs are created equal.
- When trying on a bra, lean forward and let breasts fall into the cups. This will give the fullest look.
- Your bra should feel comfortable on the center hook. That way you have some give-and-take for weight fluctuations.
- You should be able to run a finger along the underside of the straps. If you can't, the straps will likely dig in and be uncomfortable. And make sure the straps appear parallel to each other. Otherwise, it's a sign of poor construction or a bad fit.
- Women with large busts who need extra support should look for wider straps, larger fasteners, wider sides, and heavier materials, like a nylon-cotton blend as opposed to a flimsier mesh fabric.
- Bras made in France or Belgium have a reputation for quality. Of course, you'll pay a little extra for the workmanship and beautiful fabrics.
- If you want to make *big* improvements, try gel, silicone, or water-filled bras. They add extra weight (avoid the scale!) but do an excellent job of plumping up and adding cleavage where it usually doesn't exist.

- Still not enough oomph? Silicone inserts provide a natural look and are our preferred choice. You'll pay a bit more for them than foam inserts, but they feel very natural, and you can move them from bra to bra. Look for a design with nipples for added realism.
- For a boost in your bikini, try triangle foam inserts. They can be sewn right into your bikini top. But be sure to stick to thin or small inserts—too big, and they'll soak up water like a sponge and then sag.
- Aside from use in bathing suits, foam inserts are our least favorite breast enhancer. They may be inexpensive and lightweight, but they don't move with your body as well as silicone does, and foam tends to chafe.

BUSINESS SUITS

- There are good-quality suits for every budget. To stretch your dollar, remember that simple styles will stay in vogue longer than trendy fads.
- Most suits can be altered by one or two sizes, but a jacket that doesn't fit in the shoulders usually can't be fixed.
- Fabric is crucial. We like a wool-microfiber blend—which will hold its shape, resist creasing, and last a long time.
- Quality suits have a third layer of fabric inserted in the lapel, which allows the lapel to roll smoothly as well as lie flat.
- Buttonholes should be cleanly finished, and stitching should be hidden inside the lining so you don't see thread when you open your jacket.
- Lining helps clothing hang well, but it shouldn't be sewn down anywhere except in the perimeter (so at the hem and the bottom of the sleeves) and at the armholes.

> Construction and fabric, I think, are the key things in a suit. Open it and see what it looks like inside. How's the lining looking? What kind of lining [is it]? Feel the jacket, feel the fabric.
>
> **–LARS NILSSON,** DESIGNER FOR NINA RICCI AND FORMER DESIGNER FOR BILL BLASS

- Seams should sit straight and smooth across the shoulders. Make sure there is no puckering in the shoulders—it won't iron out.
- If you're buying a patterned suit, make sure the pattern lines up at all the seams.
- Want a more formal look? Go for cuffed pants. Want to make your legs look longer? Go for pants without a cuff.
- In women's suits, buy a skirt with a hemline (or have it altered) that skims one of the three areas of your leg that curve in: right above the knee, right below the knee, or right below the widest part of your calf. This will give the most slimming look.
- If you want to downplay wide hips, go for a single-breasted straight or A-line jacket. And make sure it's not too short (that is, you don't want it to stop in the middle of your rear), as that will only accentuate your hips. Slash or diagonal pockets will make your hips look smaller.
- To minimize a large bust, wear a single-breasted jacket with a deep V and avoid breast pockets.
- Double-breasted jackets can look great on small-breasted women.
- If you're petite, go for a jacket in a cropped style.

CASHMERE

- Don't get the wool pulled over your eyes! The federal Wool Products Labeling Act requires all cashmere product labels to include the country of origin, the name of the manufacturer, and the percentage of cashmere it contains. Read the label carefully. (Mongolia produces some of the best cashmere in the world, so look for that country of origin on the label.)
- A pashmina is a type of shawl, *not* a type of cashmere. If you're shopping for a cashmere pashmina, look for the specific "cashmere" content on the label. (Approximately 80 percent cashmere and 20 percent silk is a good place to start.) If the label simply says 100 PERCENT PASHMINA, there's no guarantee the item contains any cashmere at all.
- Beware of an item that appears the slightest bit shiny. That shine is probably an indication that the item is not pure cashmere.

- Ply is an indicator of thickness, not necessarily of quality. The higher the number of plies, the thicker the garment. That said, two-ply cashmere is generally more desirable than one-ply because it's stronger. Go for the warmer four- or six-ply cashmere if you're buying for cold climates—especially if you spend a lot of time outdoors.

- Hold the garment up to the light to see whether the weave is even. Consistent weave is an indicator that the piece will hold its shape.
- We're sure you'd do this anyway, but spend time touching cashmeres and comparing softness. The beauty of cashmere lies in its luxurious feel, so go for the softest you can afford.

DIAMONDS

- Buy the stone, not the ring. Buying an unset stone will allow you to verify color, clarity, and proportions in a way that simply can't be done when a stone is in a setting. The yellow or white metal color of the setting will affect the color and appearance of the stone. And when parts of the diamond are covered with claws or a bezel, flaws may be hidden from both you and the salesperson.
- Know the four Cs of diamond shopping: cut, color, carat, and clarity.
- If there's a gemologist on-site—they tend to be found only at high-end specialty jewelers—the store will have a microscope. Ask to use it to inspect any stone you're considering. The microscope will allow you to see flaws, color, and characteristics of the stone.
- If you're purchasing a diamond that's half a carat or larger, make sure the stone has been certified. Not all certifications are created equal, however. Our experts recommend

certifications from any of these independent institutes: the Gemological Institute of America, the American Gem Society, or the Diamond High Council in Belgium.

- Have the stone you're considering examined by an independent, certified appraiser (one who doesn't work for the store).
- To ensure a diamond is real, hold the stone above a newspaper. If you can read the newsprint, it's a fake.

> I've never thought of my diamonds as trophies. I'm here to take care of it and to love it, for we are only temporary custodians of beauty.
>
> **–ELIZABETH TAYLOR,**
> **OWNER OF THE 33.19**
> **CARAT KRUPP DIAMOND**
> **(AND MANY OTHERS)**

DRESSES

- There are great dresses in every price range. Make sure you check out discount and secondhand stores in your search.
- Consider the fabric. Something that is shiny is best saved for nighttime. A matte finish is more versatile in that it can work for more occasions.

- Take the appropriate shoes and panty hose shopping with you to get the most realistic picture of how various dresses will look.
- A lined dress will usually hang better. Look for flat, finished seams.
- If you find the dress of your dreams but it's too big, you might be able to have it altered. But don't buy anything that's more than one or two sizes too big. Drastic alterations can ruin the overall shape and lines of the dress.
- Got a beautiful set of ta-tas? Show them off—tastefully, of course—with a plunging neckline.
- Love your shoulders? Go strapless.

> The most important thing in dressing and beauty—and just anything—is to be comfortable with who you are. Because if you are comfortable with who you are, you will act more confident, and if you are confident, you look beautiful.
>
> **–DIANE VON FURSTENBERG,**
> **FASHION DESIGNER**

- If you want to minimize your butt or hips, choose a dress with an A-line skirt.
- A keyhole neckline is a great way to instantly enhance a small chest.
- If your arms are flabbier than you'd like, try on dresses with long sleeves or three-quarter-length sleeves.
- Going to an all-you-can-eat buffet? An empire waist will hide that bulging belly.
- If you're looking to strike a balance between sexy and conservative, go for a backless dress. Yowza!

EYEGLASS FRAMES

- Depending on the type of prescription you have, certain frames could be ruled out. Find out which frames you can have and which ones you can't before your shopping trip to prevent disappointment and help narrow down the selection.
- Plastic frames are popular, but they can become brittle over time.
- Nylon is an excellent choice of material, especially for sport glasses, as it's both strong and lightweight.
- Metals like titanium and stainless steel are durable but expensive. Cheaper metals tend to corrode from perspiration and skin oils.
- Frames made from Monel metal are a good choice. They're fairly durable, corrosion-resistant, and well priced.
- The best nose pads are made from silicone, which does an excellent job of preventing slippage.
- Look for spring hinges, which will hold the sides of the frames firmly in place. Regular hinges will loosen over time.

> In those days, you went to the optician, and you had two or three glasses to choose from—tortoiseshell or the round ones John Lennon used to wear. But now you can get everything.
>
> **—SIR ELTON JOHN** ON BUYING HIS FIRST PAIR OF GLASSES—OF MANY. BEFORE DONATING MOST OF HIS EYEGLASS COLLECTION TO CHARITY IN 2002, HE OWNED MORE THAN FOUR THOUSAND PAIRS.

GOLD

- Gold is measured in units of 24, which means that 24-karat gold is pure gold. Something that is 10-karat gold is 10 parts pure gold and 14 parts metal alloy.
- The type of alloy used determines color. The common yellow color comes from a mixture of silver and copper, while white gold gets its brilliance from nickel.
- You'll probably pay more for white gold. The price of the gold is exactly the same, but nickel (which provides the white color) is harder to work with than other alloys, so the higher price tag reflects the extra labor costs.
- Don't just go by the gold content stamp (say, 18K). Real gold will also have another stamp beside it, representing the artisan who made the piece.
- Garage-sale shopping? Don't assume you can have that gaudy necklace melted down and remade into something chic. Not all gold mixes melt smoothly, and you won't know if your mix will work until it's too late.
- Don't buy gold trinkets as an investment. Chances are the value won't change much over time, so buy them only because they're pretty!
- Be careful about buying gold pieces that are highly polished. The mirrorlike surface will show every single scratch. A matte finish is a more practical choice because it can stand up to average wear.

FAST FACT: A cube of gold the size of a plum can be beaten to form a sheet of gold leaf that could cover a tennis court.

HANDBAGS

- Beware of something stamped GENUINE BONDED LEATHER. This term means the item is made of plastic that has been treated to look like leather.
- Avoid cardboard bottoms. Sharp objects can poke through them too easily.
- Not sure if that vintage or designer bag is the real thing? Check its interior. Good-quality bags will be well lined.
- For extra durability look for straps that are double-sided— they're stronger.
- In larger bags, look for straps and handles that are reinforced with extra stitching or rivets.

- If you plan to put the handbag down on the floor, look for a protective coating or small metal feet on its bottom.
- When shopping for a bag, stuff your prospective purchase with your wallet, keys, makeup bag, and so forth. (You should see the junk Anna carries around with her!) That way you'll have a good idea of what will fit into it.

JEANS

- The best-quality denim is soft and almost velvety to the touch. It's often what's called *ring-ring denim,* or *double-ring denim.* (Check the clothing label. Some brands will list the type of denim used.) Cheaper denim is more likely to be stiff.
- Still have that old pair of jeans from high school? Today's designer jeans are softer, thinner, and more processed, and they won't last as long as that pair from your youth.
- A little bit of stretch in jeans can be good, as the denim will have "memory" and won't bag out over multiple wears. Look for a pair with 1 or 2 percent Lycra. If the jeans have a higher Lycra content than that, you'll feel like (and look like) you're wearing leggings. Perhaps not the best look. But remember that thinner denim with 2 percent Lycra will seem much stretchier than thicker denim with the same amount.

> I wish I had invented blue jeans. They have expression, modesty, sex appeal, simplicity—all I hope for in my clothes.
>
> **–YVES SAINT LAURENT,** **FASHION DESIGNER**

- If the jeans don't have any stretch, buy them a little bit snug. They'll stretch out after a few hours of wear.
- When you try on the jeans, make sure you bend and sit down in the changing room. With low-risers, check the back. Many styles gape. A lot. We say, leave the plumber look to the plumbers!
- Check the pocket placement. Pockets that are too high can make your bottom look bigger. Too low, and your butt looks like it's sliding down your legs. Pocketless styles look best on women with smaller behinds.

- To balance out wider thighs and hips, nothing is more forgiving than the boot-cut leg.
- If you're like us, you wear jeans constantly. So when you find the perfect pair, we think they're worth paying for, pretty much whatever the cost. We'd rather pay more for jeans we wear all the time than a dress we might wear only occasionally. Yes, we've spent a lot on jeans we adore—but we never regret it. (Okay, hardly ever.)

WRINKLE-FREE AND STAIN-RESISTANT PANTS

Some types of claims we just can't resist testing. After wearing, staining, and repeatedly washing numerous brands of "wrinkle-free and stain-resistant" pants, we came to a few conclusions. True to their name, these pants are only stain-*resistant* and do not repel every type of stain. In our tests, motor-oil stains did not come out. We also found the wrinkle-free feature to be more effective than the stain-resistant feature. That said, our regular *untreated* chinos looked pretty good when pulled straight out of the dryer, too. Before you wash and wear, read the labels carefully, as treated items have special cleaning instructions. And take note: Wrinkle-free and stain-resistant coatings do eventually wear off.

LEATHER CLOTHES

- The best quality leathers are *top grain*—which means the material is taken from the outer surface of the hide. *Split grain* leathers are taken from the lower surface of the hide, and aren't as strong.
- Look for aniline-dyed leathers and suedes. Aniline dye goes all the way through the skin and won't fade or show scratches as easily as will pigment-dyed leathers.
- Shopping for something tough? Go with buffalo hide. It's often used for biker gear. Cowhide is also fairly tough, versatile, and is often used for jackets. Those who want to luxuriate in softness should opt for lambskin.
- Suede should have small regular pores. Large pores are a sign of lower-quality suede.
- Make sure the dye used on your leather doesn't rub off or "spew." Test the item in the store by rubbing the leather with a tissue. The dye should not come off on the tissue.

- Check the different panels of leather. In a quality garment, the colors should match.
- As a rule of thumb, look for a lining, which will protect the leather from the oils of your skin.
- Buy your leather pants a tiny bit snug. Like jeans, they stretch over time.
- Don't use a leather protector with silicone—it clogs the hide's pores. Leather should stay hydrated, so choose a leather balm (moisturizer) protector instead.
- Tempted by bargains in a discount leather shop? Inexpensive leathers tend to come from older cows with thicker hides. The resultant leather won't be as smooth and supple to the touch as pricier pieces, and you may lose quality in the dyeing process and in the lining.

BONUS BAG:
Leather clothes can cost a lot to dry-clean. To refresh the garment without dry cleaning, pull out and hand-wash the lining, and leave it to dry outside the garment.

LINGERIE

- Lace should be smooth, not scratchy, and it should snap back into place once stretched.
- Make sure there are no loose threads hanging off the garment, a sign of lesser quality.
- Quality silk should feel heavy and drape well.
- Don't shy away from synthetic fibers. Microfiber is comfy and washable.
- French lingerie is considered among the best in the world. (Guys, if you want to impress your lady friend, think *en français*.)
- Padded bras are great for underclothing, but the—shall we say—false advertising is not so desirable for sexy

I have a lot of lingerie. After being pregnant twice, quite close together, I like anything that has a little sex appeal. Those big knickers aren't good for a girl's psychology!

–CATHERINE ZETA-JONES,
ACTOR

boudoir pieces. We recommend something nice and lacy for those steamy romantic evenings in front of the fireplace.

- If you're a plus-size woman, opt for two pieces. They're more flattering than single-piece garments, which have the potential to look tentlike.

BODY SHAPERS

Body shapers are undergarments that suck things in to reduce inches and smooth lumps and bumps. In slinky dresses and skirts, they can truly be a godsend. The higher the Lycra content, the more control you get. The range is generally 5 to 22 percent. A garment with light control usually has less control than control-top panty hose. *Medium* or *moderate* control will smooth and shape but not minimize. *Maximum* or *firm* control is designed to take inches off. But remember, to really reduce, you'll be sacrificing comfort. Choose pieces with as few seams as possible so they won't show through clothes. And if overheating is a problem for you, look for items with less Lycra and more cotton, which breathes better.

MATERNITY CLOTHES

- We know you're eager to hit the mall for new duds, but try to hold off shopping until you're at least three months pregnant. Your body won't have changed much before then. Use a belly pad to help you gauge your future size.
- With most brands, sizing is based on your prepregnancy size, so if you're normally a size 6, you'll be a size 6 in maternity clothes. And know that good-quality maternity wear is designed to accommodate you through to nine months. (Ah, the wonders of stretch fabrics!)
- Think versatility and stretch. For a sophisticated and lean look, consider dressing all in one color.
- Don't go too cheap. Yes, you're pregnant for only nine months, but you'll wear this stuff practically every day *and* in the weeks after the baby is born.

> You don't see a lot of oversized maternity clothing anymore. My biggest rule is you just never want to wear it oversized. It is very, very, very unflattering.
>
> **–LIZ LANGE,**
> **MATERNITY CLOTHING**
> **DESIGNER**

- Pregnant women get hot easily because they have more blood circulating. If you're sweating a lot, stick to natural fibers, as they breathe better than synthetics.
- Beware of low-rise pants. Our clothing testers say they don't stay up well after the belly gets big.
- Boot-cut pants are a good option for balancing out expanding hips. (This rule applies to all women, not just pregnant ones.)

PANTY HOSE

- Don't pay full price. Department stores always have sales or deals on hose—like three pairs for the price of two. Take advantage!
- Check the denier count printed on the package. The lower the count, the sheerer the hose: 10 to 15 denier is considered ultrasheer, 20 denier is for regular daywear, and 40 to 50 denier indicates an opaque hose.
- Getting the right fit for your height and weight helps panty hose last. Sizes vary between brands, so always read the sizing chart on the package. Reinforced toes and panties can also help keep hose looking their best.
- For everyday use, we like hose with 12 percent Lycra content. They are more durable, easy to put on, and maintain their shape better than hose with less (or no) Lycra.
- Expensive brands may feel silkier on account of their typically smaller stitch size, but remember, panty hose are inherently fragile. A higher price tag doesn't translate into a longer-lasting hose.

SHOPPING BAGS VERDICT: We don't like to spend too much on our hose. As long as it has a 12 percent Lycra content, you can find good-quality hose of any denier count in the midprice range.

PEARLS

- Virtually all pearls sold today are *cultured,* which simply means they're cultivated in a commercial setting. So beware of great deals on "natural" pearls; they're extremely rare and very expensive.
- There are four main types of pearls. In ascending price order they are freshwater, Japanese Akoya, Tahitian, and South Sea.

- Pearls are valued according to size, shape, color, luster, and complexion. Bigger, rounder, shinier, smoother, and blemish-free pearls are more expensive than inferior pearls.
- Ask about the *nacre* or skin of the pearl, which indicates the durability of the pearl's luster. Pearls that have been culti-vated for short periods have very thin nacre, and their luster can wear off rapidly, especially if they frequently come into contact with harsh soaps and cosmetic products like hair spray and perfume. Because pearls are a soft form of cal-cium carbonate, they're especially vulnerable to the acids contained in these products.
- If you're looking to save money, consider baroque pearls. They're a bit misshapen, so they're less expensive. We think their distinctive shapes make a statement.
- Rub a pearl against your tooth. Fakes feel overly smooth. A real pearl will feel slightly rough.
- Before you buy that necklace, check how well it has been strung by rolling it along a hard smooth surface. If they've been strung through the dead center, the pearls should roll evenly.
- Look for a necklace that has small knots between each pearl. If the necklace breaks, they won't all come rolling off.
- Consider your skin tone. Some pearl overtones work better with some skin tones than others. For example, pearls with rose over-tones look great on fair skin, while pearls with silver or yellow over-tones look best on olive skin.
- Unlike diamonds, there are no industry-wide grading standards for pearls, so their value is some-what subjective. Do some compar-ison shopping, and buy from a reputable jeweler.

> At this point, anyone can afford them, because you can't tell that much if they're real or they're fake. Wear a long strand and wrap them around your neck a couple of times. When you go with pearls, keep your earrings small.
>
> **–RACHEL ZOE ROSENZWEIG,** **CELEBRITY STYLIST (HER CLIENTS INCLUDE JENNIFER GARNER AND JESSICA SIMPSON)**

SHOES

- One in three women wear shoes that are too small or too narrow for them. Tight shoes could mean bunions in your futures, ladies!
- Shoes made of breathable material, like leather or canvas, will last longer than those made of synthetics, like vinyl or plastic. Plus, synthetic materials tend to smell over time.
- Shoes with soles that are sewn on are of better quality than shoes with soles that are glued on.
- You should be able to wiggle your toes. Look for about a thumb's width between your toe and the end of the shoe. And since most of us have one foot bigger than the other, fit the larger foot.
- Run your hand inside the shoe to make sure the lining doesn't have any seams or bumps that could cause discomfort.
- It's a good idea to shop at the end of the day, when your feet are more likely to be swollen.
- Thin soles mean more pressure on feet. Put insoles in your shoes for added shock absorption.
- Our podiatrist tells us high heels should be saved for special occasions, since they put so much stress on the foot. (We're ignoring that one, but we felt a responsibility to pass it along.)

> For me, practicality stops at about four and a half inches. Other things come under aesthetics. I'm not particularly fond of a high wedge. But I think a high heel is one of the prettiest things imaginable. As a short person—I'm five foot four inches—I count on a nice high heel.
>
> **—SARAH JESSICA PARKER,** ACTOR

SOCKS

- Feet sweat a lot. Socks made of natural fibers are healthier for you, as they allow feet to breathe better than synthetic socks, which are likely to get stinky.
- We don't recommend nylon socks. In our lab tests, natural fibers (like cashmere, cotton, and wool) were more durable than nylon. That said, don't buy 100 percent natural-fiber

socks. A sock with a small percentage of synthetic material, like Lycra, retains its shape and stays put.

- A square heel hugs the foot better than a rounded one. Rounded heels are more likely to bunch.
- The wider the band of ribbing at the top of the sock, the better it will stay up. But you don't want socks that are too constrictive; tight socks can speed the onset of varicose veins. And if the sock has Lycra, you don't need thick ribbing anyway.

- For maximum comfort, look for toe seams that sit over the toe rather than at the end of the toe. But either way, the seam should lie flat.
- Look for socks that are reinforced in the heel and toe. They'll last longer than unreinforced socks.
- Check for loose threads and uneven stitches, signs of poor quality.

SUNGLASSES

- Ultraviolet light (UV) protection is a must. Look for glasses that are tested by the American National Standards Institute or the Sunglass Association of America. (The tag or sticker will indicate whether the sunglasses have passed testing.) In our tests, inexpensive sunglasses provided just as much protection as expensive ones. And remember, just because the lenses are dark, that doesn't mean you're covered.
- Put glasses on and look at a patterned surface, like tiles, to check for distortion. The lines should stay straight when you move your head. (We have found that cheaper glasses tend to have more distortions.)
- For bright sun, green, brown, and gray lenses are considered best because they distort color least. These colors also block out most blue light, which is considered dangerous to the eye.
- Orange and yellow lenses are best for cloudy days or shaded areas.

- For very bright environments, like those with snow and water, go for polarized lenses. They help reduce glare.
- Flash or mirror lenses reflect light rather than absorb it, so they let less light through to your eyes. But they do scratch easily, so make sure you get a nonscratch coating.
- For high-intensity sports, look for polycarbonate lenses. They withstand impact better than plastic.

SWIMWEAR

- Avoid any suit made of cotton. Cotton loses its shape, fades quickly, and takes forever to dry. Polyester won't last very long either. We like a 20/80 Lycra-nylon blend best.
- Wear your tiniest undies when shopping to get the most realistic idea of what the bathing suit will look like.
- Twist, turn, stretch, bend, and squat in the changing room to make sure you've got the right fit. A well-fitting suit will shift only slightly.
- Bathing suits usually fit small, so you'll likely need to go one or two sizes larger than what you wear in regular clothes. No need to panic!
- Don't shop right after lunch when you're feeling bloated. And don't rush. Shopping for a bathing suit takes time.
- If you have a boyish figure, stick with solids, which tend to be more sophisticated than patterned or flowered swimsuits. Bandeau tops are a good choice for those with a small chest. Consider shorts-style bottoms. Just be aware that this style can make your legs look shorter than they really are. Or go for the very feminine string bikini!
- Large-breasted women will want a suit with underwire to provide support, as well as wider straps. Avoid flimsy fabrics and cuts. To minimize the chest, try color blocking. Choose a darker shade for the top than for the bottom. Do the reverse to maximize your bust (minimize your tummy or both).
- If you've got a full tummy, look for a suit with a high

> Make sure the swimsuit you buy brings out your personality. Whatever you wear should reveal your sense of self.
>
> **–BRIDGET MOYNAHAN,** ACTOR AND MODEL

Lycra content (20 percent minimum), which will help hold things in. Also, all-over printed suits or gathered or textured fabrics can help hide a belly. (Some suits even come with a hidden control panel.) Shiny or metallic fabrics will magnify the tummy.

- Got a pear-shaped torso? A one-piece suit with a low back will be flattering, as will bust-enhancing details to help draw the eye upward. Avoid a two-piece with shorts or a skirt, as that will only highlight the hips and thighs. If you want a two-piece suit, look for one with high-cut bottoms, which help elongate the leg. Also, a wide neckline will help balance wide hips.

- Find bathing-suit shopping a horrific experience? You're not alone. Try a little cognitive therapy while shopping, and focus on all the positive things you do in life (like donating to charity, taking care of a sick friend, a successful career, and so on).

TUXEDOS

- A tuxedo is considered a ten-year investment, so look for something classic. One-button or two-button tuxedo styles are considered the most timeless.

- Look for a tux in a lightweight wool or wool blend; you can wear it year-round.

- Stocky guys should stay away from double-breasted suits—they are not as flattering as single-breasted styles. And long jackets are best worn by the tall and lean.

- When renting tuxes for a wedding, do so at the end of the calendar year. If prices go up, they generally do so in the new year.

- If you're wearing a tux, there's a good chance you'll be dancing. Look for styles that have high armholes so that when you lift your arms, the collar won't gape.

- Looking for a deal? Rental shops often sell off their used tuxedos during annual warehouse sales. And ask about wedding specials. Some stores will throw in the rental cost of the groom's tux if you're renting for an entire wedding party and the bride's and groom's fathers.

UMBRELLAS

- Teflon-coated nylon is considered the most waterproof umbrella material. Plastic canopies are more commonly found in kids' umbrellas, and treated cotton can actually retain water and become heavy. (Cotton also takes longer to dry.)
- If you want a light umbrella, look for an aluminum or fiberglass frame.
- Stick umbrellas are inherently stronger than folding umbrellas.
- Check the tips of the umbrella. Look for "machine" tips, which can be pulled on and off the ribs. These tips last longer than ones that are sewn directly onto the ribs.
- Auto openers are a great feature for getting under cover quick, but they do add to the cost and weight of the umbrella.
- Look for coated ribs. A coating helps guard against rust.
- Plastic handles are more likely to crack and break than wood or rubber.
- In windy locales, look for two-ply umbrellas. One layer will be part mesh, allowing for wind gusts to pass through.
- Look for a spring coil at the top of the shaft, which allows the umbrella to snap back if inverted by wind.

UNDERWEAR—WOMEN'S

- Look for 2 to 8 percent Lycra content if you want your bikini underwear to also act as a bit of a tummy minimizer. We like 4 percent Lycra in our thong underwear for optimum comfort and longevity.
- Microfiber is a good fabric choice because it's both comfortable and durable.
- For everyday use, avoid lace. Lace underwear can be scratchy and can fall apart quickly.
- Make sure the back of your thong isn't too wide or thick, which can become uncomfortable. (Yes, comfortable thongs do exist, and we swear by them—no visible panty lines! After months of testing, we've decided our favorites come from Cosabella.)
- Don't assume sizes are consistent from brand to brand. Always try underwear on at the store (over your own, of course), because you can't return undies once you buy them.

- Check the seams. The flatter the seams, the less likely they are to show through your clothes.
- Consider low-rise underwear that won't creep up past your waistline when you bend over. (Visible G-strings are a fashion faux pas!)

UNDERWEAR—MEN'S

Boxers or briefs? We'll leave that up to you. But style aside, fabric is the most important consideration when buying men's undies. We recommend staying away from silk, which needs hand-washing. We all know guys won't wash their underwear by hand and we sure aren't doing it for them. Cotton breathes well and is soft, but it can get beat up in the dryer. If you are looking to expand the family, steer clear of tight synthetic underwear. Synthetics don't breathe well, and heat can build up, lowering sperm count. For optimum health and durability, we recommend a cotton-poly blend.

WATCHES

- There are two kinds of watches: quartz and mechanical. Quartz watches take a battery and can have digital or analog faces. Mechanical watches have analog faces and need to be wound (not the best option for forgetful people like Anna).
- If you don't like resetting your watch and don't plan to wear it all the time, stay away from one that's kinetic. It needs the movement of your arm to keep ticking.
- Although there are some fancy quartz watches out there, mechanical watches are generally more expensive because they have dozens of tiny moving parts. Also, mechanical watches can be difficult to repair. (There is actually a worldwide shortage of watchmakers and repair people—something to consider if you're looking for new job opportunities!)
- If you're a stickler for accuracy, go with a quartz watch. They keep time better than mechanical models do.
- If you have a tendency to bang into things, look for a watch with *sapphire crystal* glass. It's more scratch resistant than regular glass. Plastic scratches very easily.
- When it comes to bands, high-quality stainless steel is more scratch resistant than other alloys. It's also easier to buff scratches and nicks out of steel.

- If you're buying a waterproof watch, note the level of water resistance. For example, scuba divers will need a watch to be resistant up to a depth of 164 feet (or fifty meters). And the deeper the level of resistance, the steeper the price. Also keep in mind that waterproof or water-resistant watches won't stay that way forever. You'll need to have them re-sealed every few years.
- Fake designer watches are big business, especially fake Rolexes. To tell the difference between a real and a look-alike watch, check out the second hand. If it moves in a con-tinuous smooth sweep, it's a good bet the watch is mechanical and authentic. If it jerks from second to second, it's powered by a digital battery and most definitely a Rolex-wannabe. Also, fakes usually weigh less than the real thing.
- If you don't like to wear your watch too loose, avoid ones with large faces. The extra weight will slide around your wrist.

WEDDING DRESSES

- Begin shopping early. A special order could take three to six months. Custom dresses can take up to six months. And al-low time for a final fitting before the big day.
- Get it all in writing—the cost and everything the store and seamstress will provide, including all alterations.
- Ask the store to keep the wedding dress for you until you need it. That way the gown won't get wrinkled, and your honey won't see it ahead of time.
- Don't buy a dress that's more than one size too big. It's too difficult to effec-tively alter anything bigger than that.
- Silk is the most popular type of wedding dress fab-ric. But read the clothing label carefully. Yes, *soie* means "silk" in French, but

BONUS BAG: We invited a bunch of women over for some bubbly and asked them to wear their wedding dresses. The one piece of advice they all offered to brides? Don't worry about getting the dress dirty. Unless you, too, get invited to a wedding-dress party, chances are you'll wear it only once!

peau de soie is actually a synthetic, and its quality varies considerably.

- To save money, consider buying used. (They've been worn only once!) Buying a designer pattern and fabric and going to a seamstress can also save you about 50 percent of the price of a designer-made gown.
- Don't shy away from trying on many different styles. We can't tell you how many women we know chose styles they weren't initially considering.
- If you're full figured, try ball-gown styles.
- A-line dresses are great for hiding heavy thighs and legs. We also like strapless dresses on pear-shaped women. This style draws the eye upward.
- Sheaths are best for the slim. If you're very petite, avoid anything that has too much material. You could get lost in all that fabric!
- To enhance the bust, look for an empire-waisted or A-line dress. Also, if the style permits, you can get the seamstress to sew in breast pads.

2. Skin Deep:
Health and Beauty

Gone are the days when you can scoot into the corner drugstore for a new lipstick and a package of bandages without thinking twice about your purchases. Today, there are just so many options. Have you ever stood there, trying to spot the nondrowsy allergy medication, only to be blinded by a wall of products that are NEW AND IMPROVED! EXTRA STRENGTH! NIGHTTIME! EASY TO SWALLOW! And a simple black mascara? Forgetaboutit. Do you want lengthening, curling, or thickening? Soft black, black, or blackest black?

Fear not. Smart shopping at the drugstore is a cinch when you follow our health and beauty shopping tips. Read on, and you'll look and feel your best *and* have a few extra dollars to spend on something more exciting than TP. (Shoes! Travel! More shoes!)

> Shop at stores that have testers so you can examine color, consistency, texture, and scent before you buy.

HEALTH

A day of shopping can be hard on the joints. That's why it's critical to know which pain reliever, bandage, or antacid will cure your ailment quickly and safely. And while you can't put a price on good health, paying more doesn't necessarily get you more.

Unless you're in the market for a patented drug, we are firm believers in **buying generic** health and hygiene products. But before you buy, read the label to check the active ingredients. Ibuprofen by any other name (like Advil) works just as well. The same is true of acetaminophen (aka Tylenol).

The FDA requires generic drugs to "have the same quality, strength, purity and stability as brand name drugs." Since generics use the same active ingredients and are shown to work the same way in the body, they have the same risks and benefits as their branded counterparts.

Buying generic goes beyond drugs. Dermatologists say that all SPF is created equal. That means as long as you're buying a broad-spectrum SPF, any old brand will do. (Just be sure to check that expiration date. And dermatologists say you should use an SPF of 15 or higher.) Likewise, the active ingredients in antiperspirants are aluminum zirconium or aluminum chloride. If you want a stronger product, look for a higher concentration of the active ingredient, regardless of brand name. And tampons? The FDA defines tampons as a medical device, and as such, regulates standardized labeling terms. That means that one brand's light tampon has approximately the same absorbency as another brand's light tampon. Same goes for bandages. Our tests found that the generic brands worked just as well as name brands like Band-Aid and Curad.

Drugs and medications can be expensive. That's why many of us are turning to online pharmacies in search of a better deal. But before you buy your medications from a Web site, make sure the site is a licensed pharmacy in good standing with the National Association of Boards of Pharmacy. Buy from an illegal site and you could end up with contaminated or counterfeit products—both of which could seriously jeopardize your health.

Here's how to shop safely through online pharmacies:

- Beware of sites that offer prescriptions based only on an online questionnaire. Such forms do not replace a proper medical exam. And don't buy from a site that doesn't provide easy access to a registered pharmacist who can answer your questions.
- Some countries do not have standards and policies as strict as those in the United States. If you're buying from an international site, make sure products meet FDA approval by checking the FDA's Web site or asking your doctor.

- The FDA warns us to be wary of sites that offer "proven" or "miracle" cures. If it sounds too good to be true, it probably is.

BEAUTY

Much as we hate to admit it, we're all looking for youth in a bottle. We've all been swayed by promises of younger-looking skin, shinier hair, and fuller lips. The cosmetics aisle can suck money from your purse faster than you can say, "Reduce fine lines!" Many makeup junkies—us included—are lured by the **sensory experience**. We're talking about the beautiful jars, boxes, ribbon, scented bags, and tissue paper. But that experience is going to cost you. If all of this enhances your shopping experience, then by all means, buy away! But paying more won't necessarily get you a better product. Before you buy, ask yourself the following questions:

- How do the ingredients compare across brands? Compare the list of ingredients to those included in other products. Just as food labels do, health and beauty products list ingredients in descending order of amounts, with the first one listed being the main ingredient.
- Is the product scented? Those with sensitive or dry skin should avoid products with added fragrance, as perfumes can worsen your problem. Also, scent is one of the most expensive ingredients and can jack up the price.
- How extensive is the packaging? Packaging can account for a third of the price you pay for goods.

While the FDA regulates the cosmetics industry, it does not review or preapprove cosmetics. It only monitors product recalls that are voluntarily brought forward by the manufacturer. The FDA also does not define the vast majority of marketing buzzwords on product labels. This means manufacturers can make claims about their products that often blur fact and fiction. Your job is to read between the lines. Allow us to translate:

Cruelty-free and *not tested on animals* are not legally defined terms. They often indicate that the finished product wasn't tested on animals, but that doesn't mean some of the raw materials from other suppliers weren't safety-tested on animals. To get more information on the origins of the raw materials, try calling the manufacturer. There's often a toll-free number printed on the packaging.

Dermatologist tested does not necessarily mean dermatologist approved.

Dermatologist approved might mean approved by only one dermatologist, who may work for the company!

Dermatologically tested suggests the product has been tested on human skin. But the phrase doesn't tell you what the tests were designed to find or, more important, whether the product passed.

Hypoallergenic is used by many a manufacturer and however they see fit! Something labeled HYPOALLERGENIC suggests the product will cause fewer allergic reactions than other cosmetic products. It is not regulated by the FDA and tells you very little about the product's potential to cause allergic reactions.

pH balanced is a term most commonly used in the marketing of antiperspirants and other products that can cause skin irritation. The pH scale measures how acidic or basic a substance is. Something labeled pH BALANCED is meant to indicate that the product falls within 5.5 and 6.3, which is the same as the skin's pH range. But this term is not defined or regulated by the FDA either.

Noncomedogenic is another manufacturer favorite and another term the FDA ignores. It's meant to indicate that the product won't clog pores.

Natural. This is a growing area of the market because many of us believe natural is better; however, the term itself is used indiscriminately. Most manufacturers slap it on their labels if they've added plant extracts to the ingredient list, but that doesn't mean they've taken the synthetic ingredients out. If you see a vibrantly colored shampoo, chances are it has artificial coloring agents added. Truly natural products are much more muted in color. And it's important to know that not all natural ingredients are good for you. Menthol and camphor—the staples of many natural lip balms—are actually irritants that can make your chapped lips worse.

For sensitive skin is one claim you can usually trust. It means there probably isn't any perfume added, which is always a safe bet for people with skin sensitivities.

Contains antioxidants. When it comes to antiaging products, look for ones that contain antioxidants, which have been shown to repair and possibly prevent cell damage caused by free radicals. Antioxidants can appear in a host of forms and names, but derivatives of vitamins C and E are the most common. For more on this topic, go to "Wrinkle Cream" on page 77.

> Save the Earth! Throw that new lipstick into your purse instead of accepting that bag.

A final note on labels: When reading claims that relate to research or a study done with respect to a product, always consider the source. That is, who financed the study? Most often it was carried out by the manufacturer of the product itself, which isn't exactly unbiased research. And if you want to take matters a step further, contact the manufacturer and ask about the size and design of the study. Some products make claims like "90 percent of testers saw a reduction in fine lines." The question to ask is, 90 percent of how many? Independent dermatologists we contacted say to ask if the test results are based on a "randomized controlled trial." That means the study has included a control group, so you can more accurately measure and compare the difference the product made, if any.

So, what to do about all the false claims? Talk to the experts in your life. First stop is your doctor or dermatologist—either can help you weed through the hype about skin-care products (and makeup, for that matter). And don't forget about pharmacists. They, too, are a wealth of information right there in the drugstore. And if you've got the time, call the manufacturer (that toll-free number printed on the side of the container) and review Web sites. Finally, keep a check on your hopes of finding youth in a bottle.

What's on your health and beauty shopping list? Read on to navigate your way from aftershave to wrinkle creams and dozens of products in between.

HERE'S WHAT'S IN
OUR SHOPPING BAG

AFTERSHAVE

- Alcohol-based aftershaves are watered down and cheaper versions of cologne. So if you're looking for something with scent, aftershave is an economical way to go.
- Alcohol-based aftershaves have mild antiseptic qualities, hence the sting. And that sting isn't necessarily a good thing; a burning feeling is a sign of skin irritation. Alcohol can also be very drying, especially during winter months when skin often needs added moisturizer.
- Aftershaves without alcohol are often called aftershave balms or lotions. They're advertised as being soothing for freshly shaven skin. But most are just glorified moisturizers.
- Men with normal to dry skin should look for ingredients like vitamin E and aloe in an aftershave balm.
- Men with sensitive skin may want to stay away from aftershaves that contain alcohol, fragrance, menthol, camphor, potassium, sodium hydroxide, and anything citrus based.

SHOPPING BAGS VERDICT: To test aftershaves, we weren't going to let the boys have all the fun; we shaved our legs and applied aftershave to them. Yowza! Talk about sting! We preferred non–alcohol-based balms for their lighter scent and moisturizing properties. Our favorite was the Aveda balm, and it was the choice of our freshly shaven male testers, too.

BANDAGES

- Fabric bandages adhere to the skin better than plastic ones do, but they leave behind a stickier mess.
- Bandages should be porous to allow air to get in and out. This speeds up healing.
- Waterproof bandages are a good bet, especially for hands.
- If your scrapes and cuts tend to happen on knees and elbows, go for a brand that's extra flexible.
- Don't pay more for bandages that come with an antibiotic—a good washing will clean out your cut just fine.

- Liquid bandages are more expensive and work best on small, hard-to-reach cuts with no active signs of infection. (Think paper cuts.)
- For everyday cuts and scrapes, we recommend no-name brands. They do the job just as well as more expensive brand names.
- In our tests, we found that those "pain-free" bandages don't stick as long as regular brands do.

BLUSH

- Powder blushes work well on all skin types, but do an especially good job on oily skin. It is probably the easiest type of blush to apply, although powder tends to wear off sooner than other types.
- Gel, cream, cream-to-powder, or liquid blushes are ideal for dry skin and leave a dewy finish. But they can be a little tricky to apply.
- Do not test blushes on the back of your hand! Hands are darker and more sun damaged, and their rougher texture won't show you how the blush will blend on your cheek. Always test makeup on the area where you're ultimately going to apply it.
- Cream blushes work well with cream foundations. As do powder blushes with powder foundations.
- If you choose a powder blush, you'll probably need to buy a brush. The ones that come with most powder blushes aren't of high quality. A good brush is critical in proper application. (Go to "Makeup Brushes" on page 61 for details.)

BUBBLE BATH

- If you have sensitive skin, stick to bath oils or salts. Aveeno bath oils or Epsom salts are great choices. Our experts also recommend limiting your tub time to once a week if you're prone to eczema, dry skin rashes, or yeast infections.
- Until you're familiar with a brand, like the scent, and are confident it won't irritate your skin, buy it in small quantities. Sin-

gle portions are an inexpensive way to test a range of bath products—they're handy for travel, too!

- Synthetic surfactants (SOS) are what make bubble baths bubbly. The amount of bubbles you get relates to the amount of surfactants in a product. But use in moderation—lots of bubbles can dry out your skin.

- Some manufacturers counteract the drying effects of synthetic surfactants with other ingredients like Cocamide DEA, yet another synthetic ingredient, but one that boosts the foam, creates a more velvety bubble, and softens the water.

- Some people prefer natural or organic products because they contain fewer synthetic surfactants and preservatives. But these brands tend to have a shorter shelf life than synthetic products do. Be sure to use them before the expiration date.

- Look for hydrating ingredients, like essential oils, on the label. These ingredients will minimize any drying effect.

SHOPPING BAGS VERDICT: You don't need to spend a lot to have a great bubble bath. In a blind test, our bathers voted unanimously for an inexpensive Body Shop bubble bath over a specialty boutique brand that cost twice as much. The cheaper bubbles lasted longer, too!

CELLULITE CREAM

- They don't work, so don't bother! Believe us, we wish they did. We recommend spending your money on a pair of running shoes and taking up exercise rather than looking for a quick fix.

- The active ingredient in most cellulite creams is caffeine, which contains amanophelan. There is some scientific evidence that amanophelan can go after fat, but the caffeine content in cellulite creams is very low. And if caffeine really was the answer to cellulite, wouldn't coffee drinkers everywhere be cellulite free?

- Cosmetics companies and dermatologists are constantly working to find an effective treatment, and we're as hopeful as you are that one day they will. But before you fork over your cash, look for evidence of unbiased, fair research to support any claims.

CONCEALER MAKEUP

- The most effective under-eye concealers are yellow-ish in tone (to counteract dark circles) and one or two shades lighter than your foundation or skin.

- Here's a general rule of thumb: The drier the concealer, the more coverage it gives. So for light coverage, look for a liquid. For serious concealment, go with a stick or cream.

- Avoid concealers that are too greasy. They can cause breakouts and make laugh lines more noticeable—yikes!

- Concealer pencils aren't great for under-eye use, because they tend to tug at the skin. Save pencils for spot conceal-ment, like hiding blemishes.

- Testing the product at the store is absolutely essential for finding the right shade. If the package is closed, ask a sales-clerk to open it for you. Also, test it on your face, not on your hand. (The skin there is of a different color and texture than where you'll ultimately be applying it.)

- We're not big fans of pot concealers with multiple shades where you have to blend the color yourself. It's too hard to get it right!

BONUS BAG: While we don't know how to get rid of cellulite, we do know of a good way to help hide it a bit—self-tanning cream! We're always sure to slather some on our legs before we appear on TV in shorts or in bathing suits. For more information on self-tanners, check out page 68.

FAST FACT: Makeup artists say most women wear twice the amount of concealer they need.

CONDOMS

- Latex is an ideal material for condoms, but it deteriorates over time, so be sure to check the expiration date. Latex condoms also break down faster in warm, humid environ-ments like bar bathrooms, even if the expiration date hasn't passed. That means they're more likely to rip or break. Carry your own!

- Don't buy natural-membrane condoms. They're typically made with sheep or lamb intestine and are porous, allowing bacteria and sperm to potentially get through. Leave the intestines to the butchers.

- Allergic to latex? Go for condoms made from polyurethane.
- Don't put too much weight on labeling. The FDA doesn't regulate phrases like *extra strength*. That means one brand's *extra strength* might be the same as another brand's *regular strength*.
- A regular-size condom will fit the vast majority of men. In fact, a regular size will fit over your head. Just ask Anna—she put one over her noggin on national TV! So wise up—a condom that's too big can actually slip off at the wrong moment.
- Don't pay more for condoms with spermicide. They don't contain enough spermicide to provide any extra protection against unwanted pregnancy.
- "Thin" condoms are a good choice, as they don't tend to interfere too much with sensitivity.
- "Ribbed" doesn't make enough difference to warrant the extra cost. That's what our testers told us, anyway!

DEODORANT

- Body odor—or BO—is a tangy combination of sweat and bacteria. Aside from surgical procedures that minimize or remove sweat glands (no, thanks!), there are two ways to prevent this social no-no: deodorants and antiperspirants.
- Deodorants are like air fresheners—they mask odors your body releases when it perspires by using fragrances or perfumes.
- Antiperspirants control both odor and wetness. They contain astringents that tighten pores and block sweat ducts, as well as antimicrobial agents that kill the odor-causing bacteria.
- The active ingredient in most major antiperspirant brands is aluminum chloride or aluminum chlorohydrate. For some people, these forms of aluminum can cause skin irritation

and aggravate razor burn. To combat these side effects, some manufacturers have switched to a milder form of aluminum called aluminum zirconium tetra-chlorohydrex glycine. Check the label for it.

- Some media reports have linked aluminum in antiperspirants to Alzheimer's disease and breast cancer; however, the medical experts we asked and the FDA do not consider these products to be a health risk to consumers, because of a lack of scientific evidence demonstrating that link.

- There are a number of natural deodorants on the shelves that are made using mineral crystals or herbal compounds. They're a great option for those with sensitive skin, but they tend to have a short shelf life, so check the expiration date or ask at the store how long the product will last. (Some products like crystals may not come in packages.)

EXFOLIATORS

- There are two basic types of exfoliators: mechanical and chemical. Mechanical products contain irregularly shaped abrasive ingredients (like ground walnuts, apricot pits, or synthetic beads) that are suspended in a cream you gently rub over your face. They work by physically disrupting the surface of your skin with sheer mechanical force. Chemical exfoliators contain alpha or beta hydroxy acids and work by dissolving the bond that holds skin cells together.

- Chemical exfoliators are best for your skin because they don't tear at the skin the way mechanical ones can. This is especially true if you've got a heavy hand.

- If you're buying a chemical exfoliator and don't see the words *alpha* or *beta hydroxy* on the label, read the ingredients. Glycolic, lactic, malic, citric, and tartaric acids are all alpha hydroxies. Salicylic, tropic, and threthocanic acids are beta hydroxies.

- If your skin is oily and prone to breakouts, go for a product with a beta hydroxy. If you have dry skin, choose an exfoliator with alpha hydroxy.
- Avoid using mechanical scrubs with harsh ingredients like walnut shells, peppermint, alcohol, menthol, and eucalyptus, which can all irritate your skin if you scrub too hard. Synthetic scrubs are better because the beads dissolve as you scrub.
- Be careful of the pH level and of getting the wrong concentrations in chemical exfoliators. Alpha hydroxy products work best in a 5 to 8 percent concentration in products with a pH level of 3 to 4. Beta hydroxies are best at concentrations between 1 and 2 percent, in a product with a pH of 3 to 4.
- If you have sensitive or aging skin or are prone to rosacea or eczema, avoid exfoliators altogether. To put your best face forward, invest in a good sunscreen instead. (See "Sunscreen" on page 73 for details.)

> The product line that I value most is Kiss My Face. You can get it almost anywhere in the world. I like the exfoliating face wash and the moisturizer.
>
> **–ALICIA SILVERSTONE,** ACTOR

EYE MAKEUP REMOVER

- Shopping Bags tests revealed that all eye makeup removers work basically the same way from one brand to the next. So shop at the drugstore, and buy whatever's on sale. We like using the cheapest makeup remover we can find.
- The term *hypoallergenic* is found on the label of many makeup removers, but it isn't regulated by the FDA and is therefore meaningless. Ignore it. Same goes for *noncomedogenic.*
- If you wear waterproof mascara, choose a makeup remover with an oil base. You'll need it to get that mascara off.
- We don't recommend presoaked pads. They're expensive, and the pads are overly saturated.
- If you wear contacts (and don't wear waterproof mascara), avoid oil-based makeup removers, which can leave a film on contact lenses.

- Extra ingredients like rose or cucumber oils are just that—extra. They may feel or smell nice, but they don't add anything to the process, and you'll pay more for them.
- Avoid products with alcohol, which will dry the skin.

EYELASH CURLERS

- Buy a brand with a silicone pad, not rubber. Silicone has more spring and will give a better curl.
- Make sure the pad has a rounded edge, not a square one. A square edge will give you that oh-so-popular crimped look we'd all rather avoid.
- Be sure to buy a brand with replaceable pads.
- Avoid heated curlers, as they heat up enough to burn your skin.
- If you can, see how well the shape of the curler fits the shape of your eye. Different kinds of curlers come in different sizes.
- Individual lash curlers are good for winging out the outer corners. (They're not that good for the rest of the eye.) We suggest buying an individual lash curler only if you already have a regular one.

EYELINER

- Pencil eyeliner is the easiest type to apply.
- Liquid liners get top marks for being water resistant and staying put all day. They are, however, harder to apply than pencils. But a steady hand and practice make perfect.
- Different application methods will give different looks. A pencil or powder will give a more natural, softer look whereas a liquid liner is more defined and pronounced.
- If you are susceptible to infection, buy a pencil eyeliner. Every time you sharpen it, it's being cleaned.
- Take your time, and choose a color that complements your eye color and your skin tone. And test it out on your arm. Some liners are very waxy, and you'll have to pull at the skin to deposit color.

FACIAL MOISTURIZER

- For daytime wear, be sure to buy a moisturizer with an SPF of 15 or higher. Used daily, it's the best way to guard against wrinkles.

- If you have oily skin, look for a moisturizer that contains humectants. They will control hydration and keep the top layer of skin flexible. As a general rule, look for light, liquidy moisturizers instead of thick emollient ones. If you think your skin is too oily for any moisturizer, a well-formulated toner loaded with antioxidants might be all you need.

- Dry skin works best with occlusives, which block water loss. Look for products that contain silicone. (Note, *silicone* won't be listed on the label. Look for forms of silicone like dimethicone, cyclomethicone, and cyclohexasiloxane.)

- Normal skin? Choose a product with emollients such as squalene and cholesterol.

- Antioxidants such as vitamins C or E can also do your skin some good. But the jury is still out on whether moisturizers contain high enough amounts of them to make a significant difference in your skin's health or appearance.

> There are so many great moisturizers to choose from, but there are so many more that are a waste of money because they are either poorly formulated or just overpriced for what you get. While I am very proud of my own product line, Olay Regenerist is about as state-of-the-art as it gets and very reasonably priced.
>
> **–PAULA BEGOUN,**
> **BESTSELLING AUTHOR OF *DON'T GO TO THE COSMETICS COUNTER WITHOUT ME.***

- If you do buy a product with an antioxidant, choose one that comes in a container with a small opening, otherwise those "magic" ingredients will be promptly lost to air exposure. Alternatively, buy a highly concentrated antioxidant serum from your dermatologist, and use it along with your moisturizer.

- Avoid scented products, especially if you have dry skin. Fragrance can cause irritation and dryness.

- You don't need to spend a lot to get an effective moisturizer. In our blind tests, most of our testers choose inexpensive drugstore brands as their favorites.

FIRST-AID KITS

- Figure out where you'll be using your first-aid kit. Will it be a home kit, for the car, or for camping trips?

- Preassembled kits are generally the most expensive, but they do contain the basics. Our first-aid experts recommend starting with a preassembled kit and adding to it to reflect your specific needs (like allergies, for example).
- Cuts are the most common home injury. Make sure your kit contains at least a dozen bandages of various shapes and sizes, as well as gauze pads and adhesive tape.
- If you're buying a kit for the car or somewhere else outside the home, look for one that includes a good pair of scissors. Chances are good you'll need to cut bandages to fit a cut or scrape.
- Buy a kit that contains aloe vera gel (for burns) as opposed to burn ointment, which tends to be messy. Aloe vera is water soluble and has healing properties. If the burn is serious, you'll need to go to the hospital no matter what you use.
- An antibiotic cream is useful for cleaning out cuts and scrapes. But some doctors recommend calendula gel instead, which is an herbal disinfectant that won't promote antibiotic-resistant bacteria.
- Make sure your car kit includes matches, a flashlight (don't forget to check the batteries from time to time), flares, and something to keep you warm, like a compact foil blanket, which takes up less space than a regular blanket. We like to throw in the odd granola bar, too, just in case we're left stranded somewhere!
- The location of your car kit is key. Flares should be kept in an airtight container in the trunk. The rest of the kit should be in the backseat for easy access in the event of an immobilizing injury or rear-end collision.
- If you spend a lot of time hiking, mountaineering, and the like, choose a small, waterproof first-aid kit that can fit in your backpack.

FOUNDATION MAKEUP

- Don't test foundations on your hands! The skin on hands is darker and more sun damaged than it is on your face. Instead, test various colors by running a dab along your jawline. Then take a mirror outside with you and examine the color in natural light. And because color tends to change over time, wait a few minutes and check again. (Yes, this will indeed be a time-consuming shopping trip!)

- Yellow-based foundations, as opposed to pinks, tend to look the most natural on the majority of skin colors. Remember, foundation is not meant to add color.
- If you can't find the perfect shade, we recommend shopping at a makeup counter that will mix and personalize a color for you.
- You'll probably need to buy a couple of different shades—at least one for summer when you're tanned and gorgeous and one for winter when you're pasty (though no less gorgeous).
- If you have oily skin, look for an oil-free foundation with a matte finish. If you have dry skin, choose a moisturizing foundation. Combination skin? Liquid-to-powder foundations are a safe bet.
- If you're considering a product with SPF, find out what the sunscreen agent is. Titanium dioxide works best for most people.
- Those with sensitive skin should avoid foundation with added fragrances, which tend to sting and irritate the skin.

HAIRBRUSHES

- If you have anything longer than chin-length hair, you'll probably need two hairbrushes: one for drying and one for styling (plus a wide-toothed comb for combing out wet hair).
- If you want to smooth and straighten your hair out, buy a paddle brush, which has a flat back and a wide head.
- A round brush will provide body and curl.
- A brush with lots of space between the bristles is great for use during hair drying because the spaces act as air vents. The result is extra body and a potentially faster drying time, but you won't be able to make drastic style changes. For the most dramatic style changes, go for a brush with dense bristles that grab and lift hair easily.
- A hairbrush with a metal plate beneath the bristles can help give hair a little more body when used with a hair dryer. The metal heats up and basically acts as a roller, giving you good lift at the roots. Some manufacturers claim the warm metal helps reduce drying time, but our tests found little, if any, difference.

- Hairbrushes with plastic bristles are inexpensive, but they tend to melt under the blow dryer and break down quickly. Worn-out bristles can also cause your hair to break during styling.
- The most durable brushes are those made from natural fibers, like boar bristles. Look for boar bristles that are lighter in color at the tips (almost blond). This means the brush is made with the top part of the boar's coat, which is much softer than other bristles.
- If you're buying a round brush, the size of the barrel should correspond with the length of your hair. If you have long hair, go for a large barrel.
- Look for a hairbrush with a rubber grip. It'll help you get a grip during styling!

> **SHOPPING BAGS VERDICT:** We believe in investing in a quality brush. It's a purchase that can last years.

HAIR CONDITIONERS
- There is definitely some difference from one conditioner to the next. But the more expensive salon brands aren't necessarily any better than the stuff you buy at the drugstore.
- If your hair is colored, permed, dry, or brittle, buy either a deep conditioner or a conditioner designed for dry, damaged hair for use once a week. For the silkiest results, leave it on your hair for as long as possible. (Our experts recommend leaving it on overnight.)
- Many brands advertise different formulations for frizzy hair, curly hair, treated hair, and so on. But don't spend too much time figuring out which category you fit into. We took one brand's array of conditioners for different hair types for analysis at a lab and learned there was virtually no difference among them. We suspect this tactic is more about taking up extra shelf space than about creating a better formula for the consumers' specific hair types.
- Two-in-one shampoo and conditioners tend to weigh hair down. They're best for men or women with very short hair, who are short on time.
- If you have hard water, you may need to use more conditioner—sometimes double the amount—to get the same

level of softness you would with soft water. While there are some specialty hair products available to help combat this phenomenon. our experts say it's more economical to buy a water softener. (Not sure whether you have hard water? Look for chalky stains in your shower. Your cleansers and shampoos won't be as sudsy either.)

- Buy small bottles as you experiment with different brands. And even after you find a brand you like, be sure to switch from time to time to reduce buildup.

- For extra-fine hair like Kristina's, we recommend a leave-in spray conditioner. A light spray will help with detangling but won't weigh hair down.

> I go for drugstore stuff. Vidal Sassoon's shampoo and conditioner work really well. If it's humid, I use [John Frieda] Frizz-Ease so my hair doesn't get totally out of control.
>
> **–JULIA STILES,**
> ACTOR

HAIR DYE

- If you simply want to darken your hair for a few weeks, go for a semipermanent color. It will provide a gentle boost without the natural roots being so noticeable. But these dyes can't lighten hair, and they don't do an effective job of coloring grays. (Just ask us. Overpriced goods give us gray hair.)

- If you want more radical changes, or to lighten your hair, go for a permanent dye. It will last several months. Permanent dyes work by breaking down the hair cuticle and depositing color onto the shaft. Long-term use can be very damaging to hair, and there will be natural roots as your hair grows out, but these dyes are the best option for covering gray hairs.

- Another option is to buy an intermediate hair dye. It contains the same active ingredients as permanent dyes, but less peroxide and dye saturation. You'll need to read the label on the various boxes to compare. The change will be subtler, and it will cover about 30 percent of gray hairs.

- To add depth to hair or to color specific areas, go for highlights, lowlights, or streaks. This is a good option for the color timid among us. But we recommend going to a salon for this procedure, which takes more skill than simple dyeing.

- Overall, the products you buy at the drugstore are the same as the ones the professionals use at the salon. The difference comes in the skill of the person applying the dye. If you're going to do it yourself, you'll need practice. So don't make the night before your wedding the first time you try to color your hair.

- The difference from one brand to the next really comes down to the color choices. One brand's ash blond will be different from another's. You'll have to try several shades before you find the best one for you.

- Choose a hair dye that complements your own natural coloring. For those with eyes and skin colors in the cool tones, avoid gold, yellow, red, and bronze hair dyes, which could make you look sallow and drawn. Instead go for ash browns, cool blonds, or raven-wing black. For those with warmer coloring, go for golden blond shades, auburn hues, deep chocolates or rich browns, and avoid blue, violet, white, and jet black.

HAIR MOUSSE

- Generally speaking, mousse is a light styling aid, so it's good for those with fine hair. But it does come in heavier formulations, so look for a description of the hold on the label—it's usually described as *light, medium,* or *strong.* Some brands describe the style their product gives, like *volumizing* or *springing curls,* but as a general rule, the strength of the hold is a more consistent indicator of how the products will perform and how much control they will provide.

- While there are perfectly good brands available at the drugstore, you can save yourself the time and expense of experimenting by just using the brand your hairstylist uses—assuming, of course, you like what he or she does with your hair.

- Products containing silicone tend to make hair smooth and shiny. Look for words on the ingredients list ending in

SHOPPING BAGS VERDICT: In a blind mousse test, our testers preferred the salon brands. They said the salon brands gave them more control over the hold than the drugstore mousses and were generally more versatile.

methicone if this is a look you're going for. But silicone also makes hair slippery, so avoid it if you're looking for a stronger hold.

- Don't pay much attention to claims that a mousse contains sunscreen. Mousse that contains SPF probably doesn't contain more than an SPF 1. The amount of sunscreen ingredients that would need to be included to really protect hair from the sun would make your hair feel awful.
- Mousse that contains jojoba wax or lanolin (or both) will do the best job of protecting your hair from the elements, including the sun. Products that contain fruit juices or citric acids may smell nice, but they're less effective.

HAIR SPRAY

- Don't pay extra for salon brands! In our tests (which involved elaborate beehive hairdos and one very windy roller coaster), we found very little difference between the $2.99 hair sprays and the $25.00 brands. So you don't get a better product or better hold by paying more here.

HEALTH ALERT:

Hair sprays are a chemical cocktail, full of plastics, which can be inhaled into the lungs. (Pumps distribute fewer airborne particles than aerosols.) Be sure to use hair spray in a well-ventilated area, and don't breathe in too deeply!

- Buy small bottles until you find the brand you like; then go for the full-size bottle. (Don't forget a smaller one for your travel bag.)
- If you have fine, flyaway hair, buy a brand with strong hold.
- Each brand has a different scent, and some are quite harsh. Do a little in-store spray test to see which scents you can live with.

HAND LOTION

- Moisturizing *creams* have higher oil content than moisturizing *lotions* and are a good choice for those with seriously dry hands. Look for shea butter, lanolin, plant or animal oils, mineral oil, or cocoa butter on the label.
- If you just need light moisturizing, go with a lotion. Lotions that contain silicone do a good job of hydrating the skin without being too heavy.

- Your hands are exposed to the sun more than perhaps any other part of your body. Be sure to buy a hand lotion with an SPF.
- Some hand lotions come with antiaging claims. Look for products with antioxidants like vitamins C and E, which are believed to help prevent signs of aging. But buy a brand with a small opening, as antioxidants dissipate quickly when exposed to the air.
- If exfoliation is your goal, buy a hand lotion with poly- or alpha-hydroxyl acids.
- Look for water-binding agents on the label, which will help keep moisture in, such as lecithin, collagen, glycogen, fructose, proteins, and amino acids.
- Glycerin is a good choice if you live in a humid climate. Glycerin can draw moisture from the air and help moisten skin. But using a hand lotion with glycerin in cold, dry climates could actually speed up chapping.

FAST FACT: An astonishing 95 percent of uncomplicated skin problems are related to dehydration.

INSOLES

- You'll need to try a selection because sizes vary from one brand to the next.
- If you spend a lot of time on your feet, go for a cushioning insole. This design is intended to increase comfort.
- Stay away from latex-based insoles, which don't have the same shock absorbency as those made with Poron.
- If your feet tend to perspire, choose an odor-controlling insole. But go for one made from breathable foam, which will help keep feet dry, over insoles made from charcoal, which are designed to dissipate sweat and don't get to the bottom of the problem.

SHOPPING BAGS VERDICT: This is one test we won't soon forget. We asked a class of young ballerinas to put a variety of odor-controlling insoles into their running shoes—shoes they put on right after dance practice. Then, we actually smelled their shoes. Anna nearly passed out from the stink! (Washing your feet is probably the best defense of all.)

- Remember that insoles can help with minor problems only, like sore spots. For larger back or knee issues, you'll need to see your doctor and may have to pay for specialized orthotics for your shoes.
- Spending more on expensive insoles won't get you sweeter-smelling feet. In fact, generic brands worked just as well as name brands.

LIP BALM

- Wax and paraffin form a barrier between your lips and the environment, but they don't actually moisturize.
- The best moisturizing ingredients are emollients—plant oils (like almond or castor oil) and petroleum jelly work best. Look for them at the beginning of the ingredient list.
- Sunscreen is a must! The skin on lips is thin, has no melanin, and is therefore more susceptible to skin cancer. Buy a lip balm with an SPF of 15 or higher.
- Stay away from ingredients like peppermint, camphor, and menthol. They're irritants and can actually dry the skin. If your lips tingle, that's not a good thing.
- Don't pay more for balms with added vitamins. There are probably not enough of them in there to make a difference.
- Balms with antiseptic are good for keeping bacteria away from chapped lips.

LIPSTICK AND LIP GLOSS

FAST FACT:
Between them, L'Oréal and Estée Lauder own a large portion of all makeup lines on the market. So remember that your expensive Lancôme lipstick may have been made at the same factory as the more affordable Maybelline.

- Spending more doesn't get you a better lipstick or gloss. It's all about finding the right shade and composition.
- Shop at places where they have testers and you can try the colors. (Get the salesperson to wipe the lipstick down with antiseptic first.) We don't recommend buying lipsticks or glosses in closed packages, unless there are tester lipsticks available.
- Long-lasting lipsticks do last longer, but they rarely last all day as promised (at least not on us).

Like matte lipsticks, they are very drying. We prefer the ones that come with a moisturizing balm to use over the lipstick.

- Lip gloss is a great choice for those with thinner lips, as the shine helps make them look bigger. Don't pay more for plumping lip gloss. It doesn't work well enough to justify the higher price. Plus, they sting. And things that sting generally aren't good.

- We like lip gloss that doesn't need an applicator (or a finger) to be applied and can be put straight onto your lips from the tube. A wand applicator can get "contaminated" with color if you apply it over lipstick (as many of us do). A lip gloss that comes in a pot requires a lip brush, or it can get under your nails.

- Put the lip gloss on your fingers, and check how sticky it is. A windy day + hair + sticky lip gloss = one fine mess.

- Pigment in lipstick is a natural sunscreen. However, clear glosses do not have sun protection, so make sure you apply some sunscreen underneath the gloss.

- Avoid glosses that contain alcohol. They're drying. Get water-based or oil-based glosses instead.

MAKEUP BRUSHES

- Steer clear of brushes with blunt edges. (The only exception here being the wedge brush used for eyebrows and certain eye shadow applications.) Look for softly rounded dome-shaped heads.

- Natural-hair bristles are best for applying dry makeup products like powder blush, eye shadow, and powder.

> I look for a lip-care product that has moisturizers, sunscreen, and yummy flavors. Chap Stick offers the best products that incorporate these essential elements. My personal favorites are Chap Stick's Vanilla Mint and the Ultra 30, which has a refreshing citrus flavor and will protect your lips from even the harshest mountaintop conditions—where I spend most of my time.
>
> **–PICABO STREET,**
> **OLYMPIC CHAMPION IN WOMEN'S DOWNHILL SKIING**

- Synthetic bristles work well with wet or creamy products like foundation and lipstick.
- Brushes made from sable, goat, or blue squirrel hair have the most "grab" power (meaning they pick up the most pigment), and we found they distributed color most evenly. While these brushes are the most expensive kind, we think they're a worthwhile investment.
- The fluffier the brush, the lighter the application. (That's why powder brushes are so big.)
- Natural hair bristles fall out more easily than the synthetic kind. When shopping, gently tug on the head. If more than a few bristles come loose, go with a different brand.
- The metal band that affixes the bristles to the brush should be tight fitting. Nickel tends to provide the snuggest fit.

MASCARA

- There is no magic mascara formulation out there, so don't believe the hype. Remember that cosmetics companies don't need to substantiate claims like *thickening, lengthening,* and *curling.*
- The wand is more important than the mascara itself. The fuller the brush, the fuller the lashes.
- A smaller brush allows you to reach the corners and a comb style brush will separate bushes.
- Waterproof mascara has added wax and silicone. We recommend saving it for weddings or beach time, since getting it off can mean tugging at the delicate eye area.

MENSTRUAL CRAMP REMEDIES

- Our medical experts recommend products containing ibuprofen, like Advil or its generic counterpart. (Refer to pages 39–40 for more advice on buying generic drugs.) Ibuprofen is an anti-inflammatory *and* it blocks prostaglandin—the hormone-like substance that causes cramps.
- Some menstrual pain relievers contain caffeine to counteract the other ingredients that cause drowsiness. Keep this in mind if you're sensitive to caffeine.
- Just because a substance is natural doesn't mean it's safe. Talk to a naturopathic physician before self-medicating with herbal remedies.
- If you're looking for a nonmedicinal solution to menstrual cramps, try wearing a disposable heat patch. The thin adhesive patch relaxes muscles just as your grandma's hot-water bottle does, but it's worn under your clothing and can stay warm for up to eight hours. Our testers reported great results.
- Be sure to read dosage instructions and ingredient lists, and make note of expiration dates.

HEALTH ALERT:
Women with endometriosis should avoid heat remedies, as heat can increase menstrual flow.

MOSQUITO REPELLENT

- Study after study has shown that DEET is the most effective mosquito repellent.
- High concentrations or extended use of DEET can pose a health risk. The Centers for Disease Control and Prevention recommend using repellents with less than 50 percent DEET, while Health Canada recommends repellents with 30 percent DEET or less. Children should not use products that have more than 10 percent DEET, and it should be used sparingly.
- A high concentration of DEET does not mean better protection; it means *longer* protection. (For example, 30 percent DEET will give you six hours of protection.)
- Permethrin is a heavy-duty insecticide for use on clothing and tents. Don't buy it for use on skin.

- Eucalyptus- and soybean-based repellents can be effective, but only for short periods.
- Citronella did not perform well in our tests. (And we had the bites to prove it! To compare repellents, we stuck our arms in cages filled with hungry mosquitoes.) Some studies have also shown citronella can cause skin irritation.
- Don't use a combined sunscreen and bug repellent. The repellent can reduce the efficacy of the SPF. Plus, sunscreen usually needs to be applied more frequently than repellent.
- When it comes to mosquitoes, we don't like to mess around. (Kristina is a mosquito magnet.) We like brands like OFF and Muskol, at concentrations of less than 30 percent DEET.

MUSCLE RUBS

- Only rubs with salicylate, a relative of aspirin, have been shown to actually reduce muscle inflammation.
- Ingredients like menthol or camphor only stimulate nerve endings and give you that tingling, numbing sensation. And while that might be enough to make you feel better, know that these ingredients don't have any actual healing properties.
- Capsaicin, from hot peppers, works by disrupting pain signals to the brain. But again, it doesn't penetrate to the muscles. And most testers did not like the intense burning sensation on their skin, anyway. Go figure!
- If you can, open the package at the store, and see if you can stand the smell. Most of these products have a very strong odor.
- We found that creams were easiest to apply. Liquids with sponge applicators tended to run.
- Patches aren't as practical or cost effective if you feel soreness over a large area.

HEALTH ALERT:
That numbing menthol tingle can provide effective relief, but don't confuse it with actual healing. If you've been applying the cream for more than a week, it's time to go see a doctor.

NAIL POLISH AND NAIL STRENGTHENER

- Some nail polish contains dibutyl phthalate (DBP), a controversial chemical that has been shown to interfere with normal hormonal balance. In animal tests, exposure to large doses of DBP caused birth defects. That noted, the jury is still out on its effects on humans exposed infrequently to small quantities. If you prefer to play it safe, there are some polishes on the market that don't contain DBP—read the label.

- Nail strengtheners (and some polishes) also contain toluene and formaldehyde resins. In large doses, these substances have been shown to be toxic and carcinogenic. While they do strengthen nails in the short term, over time they can cause brittleness and discoloration. If you choose to use these products, we recommend taking a one-week-on, one-week-off approach.

- Use products that contain things like Teflon and rayon in moderation. After extended use, they can also cause some nail discoloration.

- Spending more on nail polish doesn't get you a better product. We found that expensive designer brands did not outlast drugstore brands. We do, however, tend to prefer the colors of higher-end brands.

- In our rock-climbing, dishwashing, and gardening tests, "long-lasting" polishes did not outlast regular kinds; they all came out pretty well even. (Okay, Anna went rock climbing. Kristina cowered below!)

- You don't need nail strengtheners that contain fancy ingredients like calcium or fluoride. Nails aren't like bones or teeth. They're made of keratin. So they don't need calcium or fluoride to stay strong. (They don't need keratin either, since nails can't absorb nutrients like these from the outside in.)

- Moisturizing agents can help keep your cuticles hydrated—and healthy cuticles are the key to healthy nails.

- Avoid products that contain alcohol, which can be drying.

> I'm a horrible cuticle picker. Look at my nails! If I point at something on TV, we get eighty faxes from people asking why I don't get a manicure. People are so outraged by my hands.
>
> **–KELLY RIPA,**
> **ACTOR AND**
> **COHOST OF *LIVE WITH REGIS AND KELLY***

PERFUME

- Some perfume houses use handpicked flower petals to make their perfumes. It's a very long and labor-intensive process, which is why some brands are so pricey.

- Why is something labeled *eau de toilette* more expensive than *cologne,* you ask? Because it contains more perfume oil. And the higher the perfume oil concentration, the longer the fragrance will last. In descending order of concentration, your options are perfume (15 percent to 30 percent), eau de parfum (12 percent to 18 percent), eau de toilette (5 percent to 7 percent), eau de cologne (3 percent to 5 percent), and cologne (1 percent to 3 percent).

- Knockoff or discount perfumes are made with synthetic scents. They're cheaper, but we found that the fragrance doesn't last as long as premium perfumes.

- Perfumes known as "oceanics" are made entirely of synthetic scents and usually consist of fragrances you can't bottle, like the smell of the sea or fresh linen.

- When shopping for a new scent, limit yourself to smelling three or four at a time. After that, your nose gets confused.

SHOPPING BAGS VERDICT: We believe in spending a little bit more to get a perfume you love. After all, it can become a part of your signature style and, like a watch, is something you wear every day.

- Everyone's natural body chemistry responds differently to fragrance, so when testing at the store, give the scent at least fifteen minutes to breathe on your skin before you judge it. And don't buy a fragrance based on a whiff from a bottle or how it smells on a tester card.
- Choosing a perfume is such a personal matter that unless you know the exact brand the person likes, we don't recommend buying it as a gift.

PIMPLE TREATMENTS
(OVER-THE-COUNTER REMEDIES)

- Study after study has found benzoyl peroxide to be the most effective over-the-counter pimple-treating agent, and our own tests came to the same conclusion. It kills bacteria and helps stop them from replicating. Look for concentrations of 5 percent—higher levels of benzoyl peroxide can be too drying.
- You don't have to spend a ton on your benzoyl peroxide cream—5 percent is 5 percent, no matter what the brand. Paying more may get you a nicer scent or fancy packaging, but it won't clear up zits any faster.
- Salicylic acid can also be effective for treating blemishes. It's just hard to find the right concentration and pH level in over-the-counter products, and most don't provide this information on the label. To be effective, a product needs to contain 1 to 2 percent salicylic acid and have a pH level between 3 and 4.
- Ignore terms like *oil-free, noncomedogenic,* and *nonacnegenic.* They are not legally defined or regulated terms (and not all oils clog pores).
- For a natural alternative to drugstore acne treatments, try tea tree oil in concentrations of 5 percent. But make sure you read the label, because many products contain much less tea tree oil than that.
- Steer clear of ingredients like peppermint, eucalyptus, camphor, and alcohol. They can be drying and irritating. And who needs dry *and* pimply skin?

RAZORS

- Look for a triple blade. It provides the closest shave and results in fewer nicks and cuts.

ELECTRIC RAZORS

There are two kinds of electric razors: rotary and foil. Rotary blades work better on longer hair, but they're difficult to clean. Foil razors give a closer shave and are a good choice for men who shave daily. Regardless of the type, look for a razor with at least 10,000 rpm, and remember that the more heads, the faster and smoother the shave. If you're buying a corded model, examine the cord length to ensure it will give you enough room to maneuver in your bathroom. With rechargeable shavers, check the battery life, which can vary dramatically between brands. Some last only twenty-five minutes after charging. Not great for hairy guys!

- We don't like disposable razors. Most of them come with only one or two blades. Also, by throwing them away, you produce a lot of waste.
- The main differences between men's and women's razors are the handle and the color. And yet, women's razors cost more, often due to the price of marketing and the cost of production. That's why we buy men's razors. They may not come in pretty colors, but they're cheaper and work just as well.
- Our tests found pivoting heads help avoid nicks around knees and ankles.
- We wouldn't spend more on razors with moisturizing strips that are supposed to make the razor glide better. If you use a good shaving cream or gel, you don't need a moisture strip.

SELF-TANNER

- Self-tanners are safe. The dyeing process is truly only skin deep. And it's *much* better for you than a tanning bed or sitting on the beach all day.
- The active ingredient in virtually all self-tanners is dihydroxyacetone (DHA). You don't need to buy a top-of-the-line self-tanner to get that skin-kissed glow. Focus instead on finding the right shade for your skin type and mastering the delicate art of application.
- Try before you buy. Test self-tanners by putting a stripe on your arm. Let the color develop, and see which brand you like

best. Department stores are great about allowing you to do this, and drugstores are getting better all the time. And it never hurts to ask!

- If you have normal skin, you may not need a special self-tanner for your face. However, those with oily or sensitive skin may find regular body tanner too heavy for their complexions. Finding the right one for your skin type might require some trial and error. (Anna uses body tanner on her face in a pinch, but finds that after a while it can cause clogged pores on her sensitive skin.)

> To get ready for a swimsuit shot, I usually use Decléor fake tan. It gives you great color without being in the sun—there will be no tanning beds for me.
>
> **–MOLLY SIMS,**
> **MODEL AND ACTOR**

- Many brands add fragrances to cover the slight medicinal smell of the active ingredient. But all self-tanners have some smell, even if you can't fully detect it until you're doing a more complete application.
- We like self-tanners that come in gels or creams. Sprays tend to get all over the bathroom.
- We've learned that self-tanning products have a shelf life. When shopping, ask when the shipment arrived to assure "freshness." And if you find after one or two applications that it just doesn't deliver a tan, take it back!

SHAMPOO

- Shampoo ingredients don't vary that much from product to product. The difference lies in the formulations of the same basic ingredients. Getting the right bottle for your hair involves trial and error.
- The good news is you don't need to buy expensive shampoo from a salon. Plenty of drugstore brands work just as well.
- There are claims you can trust. Shampoos for *oily, normal,* and *fine* hair provide a generally reliable guide. Also note that products for dry, damaged hair are generally identical to the ones labeled for permed or color-treated hair. These products contain emollient conditioning agents that can make hair temporarily feel less dry and damaged.

- Be wary of cosmetic promises like *adds volume, enhances shine,* or *thickens.* And don't get caught up in promises of repair. Any benefits from shampoo treatments are temporary and can't undo long-term damage.
- A shampoo should simply clean hair. Added ingredients designed to provide volume, control curl, or add shine can sometimes weigh hair down, especially if used for weeks at a time.
- Don't pay much attention to pH level; the industry standard is a pH of 5.5 to 6. While our experts say a slightly lower pH can help smooth the cuticle of your hair and enhance overall shine, hair is too finicky to maintain imposed pH levels, and styling products can counteract any possible benefits.
- *Natural* doesn't mean better. Shampoos containing plant oils and citrus extracts may smell nice, but they can also be drying and hard on the scalp.
- Don't spend more on shampoos with added proteins, amino acids, or vitamins. They don't stick to hair and just get washed down the drain.

SHAVING CREAM

- If you have sensitive skin, avoid fragranced products. Fragrance is the number one irritant in beauty and skin products.
- Men's shaving products are generally less expensive than women's shaving products, but they can also be more heavily perfumed.
- If you have dry skin, avoid shaving foams. They're loaded with soap and sudsing surfactants.
- Gels are more moisturizing than foams. And hair conditioner can work in a pinch.

- Many products contain fancy ingredients like aloe and soy. Keep in mind that these ingredients are included in very small quantities and don't spend enough time on the skin to offer serious moisturizing benefits.

SLEEP AIDS (OVER-THE-COUNTER)

- Before you buy any sleep aid, consult your doctor.
- Many sleeping aids contain antihistamines, which can be effective, but not without side effects. Antihistamines can stay in your bloodstream for up to 14 hours. The impairment is the equivalent of a 0.05 blood alcohol level.
- If you do find that antihistamines work for you, make sure you choose one designed for sleep. Some brands can have a stimulating effect, especially for seniors.
- Some people may feel agitated when taking melatonin. Some studies show that melatonin may also help people *fall* asleep but not help *keep* them asleep.
- The FDA's Center for Food Safety and Applied Nutrition regulates all supplements, including melatonin and valerian, under the 1994 Dietary Supplement Health and Education Act. This act requires manufacturers to include a "Supplement Facts" panel that outlines each ingredient in the product. Look for it.
- Before taking any over-the-counter sleep aid, be sure to read the ingredient list. Some sleep aids contain added pain relievers or medicinal ingredients for cold symptoms. Do you need these?
- There is some scientific evidence that both chamomile and lavender have weak sedative effects—especially when administered in the form of a warm chamomile tea or bath with

SHOPPING BAGS VERDICT: Our testers and our sleep specialists agree: The herbal supplement valerian is the most effective over-the-counter sleep aid. It's also one of the safest, though it should not be taken by pregnant or breast-feeding women, because its safety in these instances has not been established clinically.

lavender oil. That said, the placebo effect in sleep aids is also strong. So if you think it works for you, it does!

- Do not buy products that contain gamma butyrolactone (GBL) and gamma hydroxybutyric acid (GHB)—they have been shown to cause serious side effects, including death.

SOAP

- All soaps are remarkably similar. They contain a vegetable oil or an animal fat, plus an acid and a base. These basic ingredients work together to create suds.
- You'll pay more for a nicely fragranced soap, but it won't clean any better.
- If you want a moisturizing soap, look for ones with cocoa butter, shea butter, or castor oil. But remember that most moisturizing ingredients do just wash off down the drain. It's better to moisturize separately.
- Vitamin- or mineral-enhanced soaps generally don't contain enough of these ingredients to do any good.
- For sensitive skin, look for soaps made from pure glycerin. They don't contain any animal fat, which can be too harsh for some skin.
- *Superfatted* soaps have more fatty substances in them like coconut oil or lanolin. They aim to be more moisturizing, but we find they tend to leave an oily film behind.
- Castile soaps are made of olive oil and water, and are virtually unscented. Though on the greasy side, this kind of soap is ideal for very dry skin.
- *Triple milled* means the soap has been pressed three times to eliminate air. This means a denser, albeit pricier soap, but it will last longer.
- Deodorant soaps are loaded with harsh additives that kill odor-causing bacteria. While these bars smell sea-breeze fresh, they can be

HEALTH ALERT:
The Centers for Disease Control and Prevention recognize hand-washing as one of the most important ways to prevent germs from spreading. A good washing should take at least thirty seconds, and it should be done several times a day.

drying and irritating to the skin with prolonged use. Use milder soap for cleaning, and apply deodorant after you shower.

- We don't recommend using antibacterial soaps in the home. They can help create germs that are resistant to antibiotics.

SUNSCREEN

- The number one Shopping Bags beauty rule: You must buy and wear sunscreen!
- For the best protection from ultraviolet rays, buy sunscreen that has a sun protection factor (SPF) of at least 15. An SPF of 15 provides 95 percent protection from UV rays, while an SPF of 30 provides 97 percent protection.
- When you buy an SPF, take into account how long you plan to stay in the sun. For example, an SPF of 30 will let you stay out for twice as long without burning as an SPF of 15 will. Or thirty times longer than if you didn't wear any sunscreen at all.
- Make sure the label says *broad spectrum.* That means the bottle supplies both UVA and UVB protection.
- Look for the American Dermatology Association logo. It's presence means the sunscreen is up to standard.
- Once you follow the above rules, all sunscreen is created equal. That means a ten-dollar broad-spectrum SPF 15 sunscreen, approved by the ADA, will provide the same protection as a thirty-dollar bottle. However, you may prefer some brands over others for their texture or scent.
- Look for a water-resistant protection if you will be swimming and sweating.
- Be wary of too-good-to-be-true terms like *all-day protection* and *waterproof*—no sunscreen can live up to such claims.
- Sunscreen has a limited shelf life. Check the expiration date.

BONUS BAG: Apply more sunscreen than you think you need—it takes a shot-glassful to cover an average-size body. Most people put on half as much as they're supposed to. Sure, it can be a hassle, but remember, 90 percent of your wrinkles are caused by sun damage. We think that's a great motivator.

TAMPONS

- Most women don't use the right size tampons. Use the least absorbent one you need. If the tampon isn't saturated in three to four hours, it's too big. And taking it out while it's still dry could cause tears to the skin.

- The FDA has standardized tampon absorption. So regardless of brand name, all *junior* tampons will absorb the same amount. Same goes for *regulars, supers,* and *super pluses.*

- We like multipacks that contain various sizes of tampons. You'll pay more for these packs, but this way you'll have the right absorbency on hand throughout your cycle.

- Check the shape of the tampon. Our testers found that long and lean tampons (like those made by Tampax) are more comfortable to remove than ones that expand too much in width.

- Dioxins are bleaching agents used to make tampons white. Most health experts, including the FDA, say the quantity of chemicals used is too small to be of concern. But you can buy organic tampons. They're made with 100 percent pure cotton, and don't contain bleaching agents or other chemicals.

- A paper applicator is more environmentally friendly than a plastic one.

TEETH WHITENERS

- Over-the-counter teeth whiteners can only make teeth two to four shades lighter.

- Look for products that contain 10 percent carbamide peroxide (which is the equivalent of about 3 percent hydrogen peroxide). The higher the concentration, the whiter your teeth can get. But high concentrations can also result in greater teeth sensitivity.

- In our tests, strips were easy to use and got teeth whitest.

- Paint-on formulas are easy to use, but testers found it difficult to determine how much to put on and, in the case of clear formulas, how much they *had* put on.

- Trays are cumbersome to use and not good for those with sensitive teeth and gums.

- Bleaching trays that your dentist custom-makes for you are more effective than store-bought trays. They fit your teeth exactly, and you'll have less chance of swallowing the peroxide (which can cause a sore throat and upset stomach—plus it tastes lousy).

- Spending more does not get you whiter teeth. Drugstore brands did just as well as or better than "designer" brands.
- Yellow or brown teeth are most receptive to bleaching. Gray teeth or those stained by tetracycline may not whiten at all.
- Most whitening toothpastes contain abrasives. Those with peroxide contain such small amounts that it takes a long time for any visible effect to occur.
- Laser whitening is the most effective (but also most expensive) way to whiten teeth.
- Whitening floss will not bleach teeth. Don't bother unless it encourages you to floss more!

THROAT LOZENGES

- Various lozenge brands use different key ingredients, including numbing oral anesthetics, to make your throat *feel* better temporarily. But our medical experts tell us they won't heal your sore throat.
- Herbal lozenges, like those containing mint and eucalyptus, have a cooling, soothing effect, but again, they don't treat the cause of the ailment.
- Some medicinal lozenges claim to be antibacterial. Sore throats are often viral, not bacterial. And no lozenge can target the exact type of bacteria in your throat—there are just too many different strains out there.

HEALTH ALERT:
There are some health concerns with taking zinc. It can cause stomach irritation, nausea, and vomiting, and should not be taken by those with ulcers.

- Most lozenges contain a lot of sugar, and sucking on them can be just as bad for teeth as sucking on candy. Opt for sugar-free.
- Zinc lozenges are supposed to shorten the duration of a cold and thereby a sore throat. The medical jury is still out on whether they work or not.
- Our verdict? If it makes you feel better temporarily, go for it!

TOILET PAPER

- If you want strong toilet paper, go with a no-name brand or an environmental brand. Though on the scratchy side, they'll do the job just fine. If you prefer soft toilet paper, go with a brand name.
- Recycled toilet paper is rarely made with 100 percent recycled product. Usually it's between 10 and 40 percent. Read the fine print.
- Yes, on average, you get the number of squares listed on the package. We counted!
- When comparing quantities, not all brands make the same size squares. We found that some no-name brands have smaller squares than brand names.
- When it comes to TP, we don't keep an eye on the bottom line. We like the brand-name stuff—it's usually more absorbent, so we use less. Plus, we like the softness!

TOOTHBRUSHES

- Dentists recommend a soft- or ultrasoft-bristled toothbrush. Medium and hard brushes are too rough on gums and tooth enamel.
- Look for a long handle and a small head. These features make reaching back teeth easier.
- Rounded bristles are softer on gums than angular bristles.
- You don't need to spend a lot to get a quality brush. Your brushing technique is more important than the right brush. (Most people brush too hard and not for long enough.)
- Electric toothbrushes with timers can be a good investment for those people who don't brush long enough. However, we find these toothbrushes can easily break down because of all the water and paste that gradually builds up inside the motor.
- In our tests, electric toothbrushes did a slightly better job of removing plaque—probably because testers used them for longer.

HEALTH ALERT:
The average American brushes for forty-five to sixty seconds. Dentists say you need to brush for at least two minutes for effective cleaning.

TOOTHPASTE

- Good toothpaste should contain abrasives to clean teeth, antibacterial agents to fight plaque and gum disease, antitartar agents to prevent tartar buildup, and fluoride to prevent cavities and decay. A good bet is to go with one that says *Total* or *Complete*.

- Look for the American Dental Association's seal of acceptance. The ADA seal means the toothpaste has been reviewed and deemed safe and effective.

- Tartar-control agents like pyrophosphate do not remove tartar. They can only prevent it from building up in the first place.

- Triclosan is an antibacterial agent. It's added to some toothpastes to fight bacteria found on the gums and help prevent gingivitis and plaque buildup. Many dentists recommend using a toothpaste with triclosan as a preventive measure, so look for it in the ingredients list.

HEALTH ALERT: Too much fluoride can cause dental fluorosis—a cosmetic condition where white specks appear on a child's teeth. Consider using a fluoride-free toothpaste on children under three, and use only a pea-size amount of any toothpaste on their young teeth.

- Whitening toothpastes contain abrasives that can remove stains, but they're not so effective at whitening teeth overall. (See "Teeth Whiteners" on page 74 for more on this topic.)

- If you have sensitive teeth and gums, look for toothpaste that contains strontium or potassium nitrate. Both are desensitizing agents recognized by the ADA.

- Baking soda is a mild abrasive. Prolonged use can lead to some irritation.

WRINKLE CREAM

- There is no miracle cream on the market. Do not believe the hype! If there were, why would cosmetic surgery be on the rise?

- Retinol, a type of vitamin A, has been shown to have some effect on wrinkles. Renova and Retin A are similar ingredients, though available only through prescription.

- Alpha hydroxy acids (AHAs) are exfoliants that slough off the top layer of skin and moisturize what lies beneath. This can

> If you're starting to worry about wrinkles (or if you're smart enough to plan their prevention), add an antioxidant-rich anti-aging serum into your nightly skin treatment schedule, applying it after your toner and under your moisturizer. Regular use will keep lines on the lam.
>
> **−MARCIA KILGORE,**
> **FOUNDER OF BLISS SPA**

help reduce the appearance of wrinkles, but seems to work best on younger skin. Most OTC products contain between 3 and 7 percent AHAs, but they work best in concentrations of 5 and 8 percent and in products with pH levels between 3 and 4. If this information isn't indicated on the label, ask a store clerk for help. Some products contain as much as 20 percent AHAs, but don't begin using those until you've consulted your dermatologist.

- Any daytime antiwrinkle cream *must* contain a broad-spectrum sunscreen with an SPF 15. Using sun protection is the only real way to *prevent* wrinkles from forming.

3. Feathering the Nest: Furniture and Home Decor

Your home is your sanctuary. Whether it's a rented shoe box apartment in the East Village or a sprawling mansion in Beverly Hills, you want it to be beautiful, functional, and comfortable. For most of us, that's an ongoing process! Fortunately, we've learned some tricks for making the perpetual search easier:

Negotiate! Furniture pricing is based on the cost of materials and the workmanship involved in constructing it. And that is about as specific as we can get—the range of prices out there is absolutely staggering. But as with all other major purchases, we heed Commandment #1 and negotiate. If you can't get a lower price and can't afford to pay full pop, see if they're willing to sell the floor model. The minor wear and tear from customers usually results in a better deal. You can also ask when floor models go on sale. If they're still not budging, ask to get delivery thrown in for free. A furniture store Kristina was dealing with finally relented on this point, and she saved over sixty dollars on a buffet.

If you're buying something large at a garage sale and need to go away to arrange for delivery, take a drawer or other such piece of the item with you so the seller doesn't resell it before you return.

Read those hanging tags. It may look like solid wood, but how do you know it's not a cheaper veneer? Knockoffs and cheaper imitations abound in the furniture industry. There are some ways to assure you're getting quality. It's a federal offense to misrepresent the materials used. If the product is made with veneer, it must say so on the label. We always look for a hardwood frame (like maple, alder, or oak) as opposed to plywood or softwood. Hardwood costs more, but it will stand the test of time.

Buy direct. Check to see where the item was made. If it's made locally or nearby, you might be able to buy directly from the manufacturer at a better price. Like the time Anna got her farmhouse-style mirror at a fraction of the boutique's price, simply by looking up the name of the manufacturer in the phone book. It's worth a try!

Warning: Objects in showroom are larger than they appear. Always, always bring a measuring tape with you, and be sure to measure out the space you're looking to fill at home beforehand.

Warranties. Almost all new home furnishings come with one, but some guarantees are better than others, so you need to read carefully. In general, warranties won't cover everyday wear and tear or "improper use," but they will cover defects in workmanship, materials, and construction for anywhere between three and twenty-five years. But every component has a different guarantee and a different expiration date. Frames and springs are usually guaranteed longer than cushions, fabrics, and zippers. For example, Ethan Allen warranties the frames and springs on its sofas for seven years, but zippers are covered for only three—and tailoring defects have to be reported within ninety days of delivery! Bottom line: How much stock you put in the warranty will ultimately depend on how long you need the furniture to last. (Do you have young kids? Is it a light-colored couch?) Think about how heavily it'll be used.

Additional protection. Does your new couch need extra stain protection? If Scotchgarding isn't included in the price, negotiate for it. That said, our experts agree that a good spray you can buy at a drugstore will do the job just as well. You'll just have to be diligent about applying it.

In-store designers. Take advantage of them! National retail chains like Bloomingdale's and many independent furniture stores offer the services of trained designers at excellent rates. Sometimes design service is even free with a purchase, regardless of how much you spend. It's definitely worth seeking out.

Unless you know exactly what you're looking for—down to the make and model—we don't recommend buying large pieces of furniture online. It's important to assess quality by examining items in person. Plus, sitting and lying on chairs, sofas, and beds are a must!

Zero money down. We've all seen advertisements at furniture (and electronics) stores: BUY NOW AND PAY LATER, NO INTEREST! But be aware that some of these programs do have additional administrative fees or may require you to use an in-store credit card, which typically comes with a higher-than-usual interest rate. If there's any chance you won't be able to afford the item when the deadline comes around, we recommend avoiding "zero deposit, zero interest" programs. Heck, we prefer to just save up and buy when we can afford to pay. Call us old-fashioned.

But furniture is just the beginning. It takes a lot more stuff to turn a house into a home. At some point in your life, you'll probably have to buy most of the following essential items to feather your nest. And if you follow our shopping tips, you'll never have to sleep on a lumpy mattress with scratchy sheets, snuggle on a sagging sofa, or sniff toxic candles again!

HERE'S WHAT'S IN
OUR SHOPPING BAG

ANTIQUES

- Antique furniture has the highest incidence of fakes, and early glass pieces tend to be the most rare.
- Pieces are usually classified by country of origin and date, as well as the reigning monarch of the time (like "Queen Anne" if English or "Empire" if French—but watch out for something labeled "Princess Shopping Bag").
- Haggling is expected even when you're shopping at an antiques dealer.
- A dealer can be a great source of information, and many will let you take a piece home on a trial basis. Take them up on it.
- If shopping at a dealer, your receipt should contain more information than just the price. It should also outline period, type of piece, and information about where it comes from. That way, if it turns out to be a fake, you might have some recourse.
- Auctions can be a good place to shop. But remember that every item is sold as is, and all sales are final. Be sure to attend the presale to preview items up close.
- Check your local newspaper for estate sales. They can be a great place to nab deals, as the seller is typically eager to get rid of items.
- Garage sales can be a good place to shop for antiques. Show up early, but not too early. Most garage sale holders don't appreciate shoppers showing up before the posted opening time. Cash only, please!
- No matter where you shop, take a flashlight to closely examine the piece and determine its condition. Look at it from all angles, pull it away from a wall, and pull drawers out all the way.

> I won't go to a flea market with David [Arquette] ever again, because he likes to stop and see every little piece that's on each table. Me, I'm like radar; I go straight to what we need or things I'm attracted to. I don't sift through very well.
>
> **–COURTENEY COX ARQUETTE,** *FRIENDS* **ACTOR, AND PRODUCER OF THE DESIGN SHOW** *MIX IT UP*

BED LINENS

- Don't put too much stock in the label. It doesn't necessarily reflect what's in the package. Only buy sheets you can actually feel before you buy.

- Thread count is a measure of the number of threads per square inch. This can range from around 180 to over 1,000. A higher thread count can mean a softer sheet. Most people are satisfied with a thread count between 180 and 300. But thread count alone does not make for a soft sheet. The type of cotton used also comes into play. So be sure you open that package and feel.

- Egyptian cotton is grown on trees as opposed to bushes and produces longer threads that create a smoother, softer weave. It's also more expensive than regular cotton. If you're going to spend the money on Egyptian cotton, make sure it's a long staple yarn that has been combed, woven in Italy, and has a high thread count.

- A cotton-polyester blend isn't as soft as pure cotton, but it's easier to care for and resists wrinkles. Polyester reduces shrinkage and dries faster.

- Sateen is considered to be the most luxurious fabric for sheets. Not to be confused with satin sheets (which are all polyester), sateen sheets are 100 percent cotton, are specially woven to have a slight sheen, and are more delicate than cotton-polyester blends. They won't stand up to everyday wear and tear very well unless cared for properly. But they feel divine!

- Linen and silk are great if you live in a hot climate. These sheets will last for decades but do require special care.

SHOPPING BAGS VERDICT: To find out if people can tell the difference between low- and high-priced sheets, we made up four beds in a department store and asked shoppers to dive under the covers. (One eager fellow even took off his shirt!) Almost everyone preferred the soft and luxurious feel of our thousand-dollar Egyptian cotton sheets. Unfortunately, everyone also admitted they could never afford them. The runner-up was $276 Indian cotton. Not cheap, but at least it's in the ballpark!

Linen sheets will also need to be ironed, unless you like the shabby-chic look.

- Department store sheets are always going on sale. Don't pay full price.
- Modern-day mattresses have become much deeper. Make sure your new sheets can accommodate the size of your mattress. Look for deep pocket measurements—those that fit up to a 15-inch mattress.
- If you can, hold sheets up to the light in the store. Better-quality cotton will appear even and smooth, whereas lesser-quality cotton looks lumpy and inconsistent when held up to the light.

BLINDS

- If you can afford it, go for custom-made blinds. They'll cost you a bit more but will provide the best coverage for your windows.
- If you buy ready-made blinds from a home-improvement store, the cost of cutting them down to your specs is usually included. If you shop at a department store, you may need to take your blinds elsewhere for sizing. Be sure to factor this alteration into the overall cost.
- Before you go shopping, measure the top, middle, *and* bottom of the inside of the window frame. If the numbers are inconsistent, go with the smallest of the three.
- If keeping out the light is important to you, go for thicker slats. Fewer slats means fewer openings and therefore better coverage. We think light blocking is a must in the bedroom.
- Look for mechanisms that are metal on metal. Plastic parts won't last as long.
- If you have small children, look for blinds that come with a breakaway tassel to eliminate any risk of strangulation.
- Faux wood blinds are cheaper than the real thing, but they're also heavier and require a little extra strength to open and close.
- Vinyl and faux wood slats (as well as extra thin wood slats) can warp over time if your window receives a lot of direct sunlight.

CANDLES

- Candles have trustworthy labels! In our burn tests, most lasted as long as promised.

- Beeswax candles will burn more slowly than the lower-priced, more-common paraffin candles. But make sure the label says 100 percent PURE BEESWAX. If it says only BEESWAX or PURE BEESWAX, it might only be 51 percent beeswax, while the rest is paraffin.

- Metal wicks made of lead are a health concern and should be avoided. To find out if a wick has lead, cut off a small piece of the wick and unravel the outside coating. Rub on some paper, and if it writes like a pencil, you know you've got a lead wick. Lead wicks are becoming less common, but you're more likely to find them in inexpensive tea light or votive candles, rather than in tapers.

> It's important not to burn candles that have a heavy scent—like rose, vanilla, or patchouli—on the food table, because it can mask the smells of the delicious food being served and disturb your guests.
>
> **–MICHELE ADAMS AND GIA RUSSO,** AUTHORS, EVENT PLANNERS, AND HOSTS OF *MIGI* ON THE FINE LIVING NETWORK

- Some people find that artificially dyed or scented candles cause headaches or eye irritation over time—even candles containing more natural essential oils can irritate the sensitive candle consumer. So check the label for a list of ingredients if this is a concern.

- The right wick will help your candle burn slowly and evenly. Braided wicks, not twisted, are best. Some manufacturers even distinguish between square-braided or round-braided wicks, but there's little difference—just look for good tension.

- To avoid the dreaded sunken wick, burn candles for at least an hour, or until you see the walls of the candle shine with melted wax.

- Be aware that scented candles can produce more soot than unscented ones.

- If you're still disappointed with your candle's burning performance, take it back. It's standard practice at specialty candle stores to return or exchange dud candles.

CHINA

- Don't buy or register for a pattern that's about to be discontinued. Inquire about how long the pattern has been in production and how popular it is. If your pattern does get discontinued, keep in mind that many specialty shops keep stockrooms full of old patterns.
- If you can't decide on a color or pattern, go with a simple white or ivory (but with a simple pattern so it's not too boring). You can add colored pieces later.
- Hold a plate up to the light. A dish made of fine china will allow you to see the shadow of your hand behind it.
- Flick the edge of a dish. It should resonate.
- Check the quality of the glaze by running your fingers around the outside of the dishes. Look out for bumps or cracks.
- Try to choose a pattern that sells "open stock" pieces so you don't have to buy a complete place setting every time you want to add to your collection.
- Plates with silver inlaid along the edge are not dishwasher safe—the silver can scratch and tarnish. Handwash the dishes in warm soapy water with a soft cloth only.

CHRISTMAS TREES (THE NATURAL KIND)

- If you have a cat, choose a spruce tree. They have prickly needles, so your kitty won't meddle with your decorations. These trees have poor needle retention, though, and won't last very long.
- Douglas fir trees are a good choice for needle retention and price.
- If it's an aromatic tree you're after, consider the grand fir. But it will last only about ten days because its needle retention is poor.
- If you want your tree to last as long as possible, go for a noble fir or fraser fir. You'll pay more, but your tree will be around for weeks.
- To check for needle retention in the lot, grab a bunch of needles, and gently pull. If several come off in your hand, the tree may have low needle retention. If a lot fall off, the tree is likely dried out. Choose a different tree.
- When buying from a lot, inquire about where the trees come from. A locally grown tree is likely fresher and will last longer.

COMFORTERS AND DUVETS

- The first consideration is whether to buy a down-filled duvet or synthetic comforter. Down is more expensive, but it will last longer. It is also more breathable and adapts to body temperature better than synthetic fill.
- The most expensive down comes from Hungary, Siberia, and Poland. The cheapest comes from China.
- If you go the synthetic route, look for cluster polyester. It's light and airy and feels a little bit like down.
- Wool-filled comforters are another option, but check out the weight, as they tend to be heavy.
- Squeeze the comforter in the store. Something that's of good quality will quickly bounce back.
- Look for the "fill power" or "loft power" (the measure of a comforter's ability to hold air) on the label. Generally speaking, the higher the fill power, the better the duvet (A fill power of 550 is considered good quality, but it goes as high as 850.)
- The casing on duvets is also important, as poor-quality casing could mean a "leakage" of feathers. Ensure it's "down proof" and made from good-quality cotton with a high thread count (at least 220). But don't just depend on what you read on the label; be sure to actually feel the product.
- If you're buying a duvet, choose one made with box stitching, which helps the down to stay in place. Channel designs allow the fill to get all bunched up at one end.

SHOPPING BAGS VERDICT: Whatever type you choose, we believe this is one product that's worth investing in. We all need our beauty sleep! Anna swears by her down duvet, and after our sleeping tests, Kristina is a cluster-polyester convert. It has the light airy feel of down and doesn't make her sneeze!

CRYSTAL

- For something to be deemed true crystal, it must contain lead. That's what gives it its unique translucency and clarity. There are many products available that call themselves "leadless crystal" but without the minimum 10 percent lead content, it's really just glass.

- The price you pay often depends on how the crystal is made. The price tag is higher for a glass that's mouth-blown and hand-cut versus one that's machine-made.
- You may also pay more for seemingly plain crystal items. This is because they're difficult to make. Plain thin crystal will show flaws more easily than a detailed item that could simply have a bubble cut away, which means the cost of manufacturing can be high.
- Examine the clarity of crystal pieces. Superior quality will have better clarity.
- You can tell a crystal wineglass has been handmade when it doesn't have a seam between the bowl and the stem.
- If you're just starting your crystal collection, start with water goblets and wineglasses. That way, you'll have the basics covered for entertaining.
- When choosing a pattern, be aware that some are much more susceptible to breakage—especially ones that are extra thin or curve out at the top in a tulip shape.
- Don't worry too much about your pattern being discontinued. This phenomenon is much more common with china.
- Some insist that wine tastes better out of good-quality crystal. But we say wine tastes great out of any kind of glass—even a Styrofoam cup!

BONUS BAG: The best way to clean your crystal is with hot water and a little vinegar. And wash them one at a time to avoid any chipping.

DESK CHAIRS

- Look for a chair with adjustable height, backrest, and arms.
- Fabric used to make the chair is important. If you can easily poke a ballpoint pen through the upholstery, the weave probably isn't sturdy enough for daily use. The tighter the weave, the tougher the fabric.
- Leather is a durable option, but it's expensive and could get sticky during the summer months. Chairs made with fabric upholstery have a lower price point, but they probably won't last as long as leather or vinyl.

- Make sure the front of the seat slopes downward (referred to as a waterfall edge), which is said to improve the circulation in your legs. Some chairs even allow you to adjust the seat edge angle.
- Sit in the chair in the store to test for comfort, and make sure you can reach all the adjustments from a sitting position. Some stores will let you take a chair home for a trial run.
- The backrest should be contoured to provide lower-back support and should be separate from the seat.
- Look for a five-point stable base with a swivel mechanism.
- WARNING: Desk chairs in the store will inevitably feel more comfortable than the one you're currently using, so don't jump at the first chair you try! Test a number of them so you have a basis for comparison. And remember, a good chair should feel comfortable five years from now—so look for good-quality construction and materials. Your back will thank you.

FLATWARE

- The first thing you should look at is the fork. Tines should come to a fine taper and be pointy enough (but not sharp) to easily pierce small pieces of food.
- Look for a spoon with a deep bowl and smooth edges.
- Hold the pieces in your hand. Make sure they fit well and are balanced.
- Silver-plated flatware will probably last your lifetime, but not your children's. If you want something to pass on through the generations, you'll have to buck up for sterling.
- Good-quality stainless-steel flatware will have the numbers 18/10 stamped on the back of each piece. The first number reflects the percentage of chromium, which prevents your flatware from

Many brides are registering for stainless-steel flatware instead of sterling. They want to throw it into the dishwasher. They want ease of use. And there are such pretty patterns that I think it is perfectly appropriate.

–MARTHA STEWART

rusting, and the second refers to the nickel content for shine and strength. Lesser-quality flatware will have a lower nickel number.

- Ten place settings are usually enough for most people. Buying ten settings can be difficult if you're buying less expensive stainless steel, however. It tends to come in boxed sets of four or eight.
- Find out if the pattern you're considering comes with serving pieces. Many stainless-steel patterns do not.
- Most people we asked agreed that flatware is worth spending a bit of money on. That way you get something that looks and feels nice and will last.

LAWN FURNITURE

- Cedar and teak are good low-maintenance options, as they can be left outside without special care.
- Wicker or rattan is usually made from light wood. It's easy to move, but it can't be left outside for long periods of time. It's best suited to sunrooms or covered patios.
- If you really like the look of wicker outside, opt for hardier resin-coated fiberglass-molded wicker, aluminum wicker, or the pricey Hularo fiber wicker from Denmark, which is specially color treated to reduce the appearance of scratches.
- If you want to buy metal furniture but are worried about rust, go with cast iron or the less expensive cast aluminum.
  - Wrought iron is cheaper than cast iron but can rust if scratched, so make sure it has a protective coating on it. (Or, coat the metal with paste car wax instead! Refer to "Car Wax" on page 211 for details on how to pick a good wax.)
  - With metal furniture, look for feet that are raised off the ground with small pads. The pads will keep the feet out of puddles and prevent rust damage. If the furniture is going on the lawn itself, look for legs with flat wide feet that won't sink into the soil. And if

BONUS BAG: While the latest patio cushion fabrics are more resistant to rain and moisture damage, they'll still take a few hours to dry out completely if they get caught in the rain. To keep them looking their brightest, store them indoors and out of the sun between uses, and clean them with a mild upholstery shampoo as needed.

it's going to go on uneven ground, look for screwed-in foot-pads that can be adjusted for height.

- For outdoor cushions, look for a special outdoor acrylic or acrylic-blend fabric with a fibrous—not foam—padding. Instead of being water repellent like other fabrics, outdoor acrylics allow water to run through and are much more breathable. This makes for a quick drying time.

- Get a lawn umbrella with a sturdy base to withstand high winds—especially important if you're using your patio furniture on waterfront property. A base for a small umbrella should weigh at least thirty-five pounds, while standard-size eleven-feet-tall umbrellas need one that weighs in at seventy pounds. Also look for ventilation slits at the top of the umbrella, which are usually covered by a loose fabric skirt.

- On all types of lawn furniture, look for hardware made of stainless steel or marine-quality brass. Inexpensive steel fittings can rust, and cheap brass can turn black and the brass color can actually run.

MATTRESSES

- Never pay full price. There's lots of room to negotiate on mattresses, and they always go on sale. If the store won't reduce the price, ask for free delivery. (When Kristina bought her mattress, she got them to throw in a metal frame, a mattress cover, and delivery.)

- Generally speaking, more coils mean more support. But be sure to check the coil *gauge*, as well. Thick coils give more support than thin ones. The lower the gauge number, the thicker the coil.

- Look for padding above the coils that's made of convoluted foam. (It looks like an egg carton.) This type of foam helps distribute weight better than flat foam. And if you can, check that the foam doesn't feel dry or crunchy, as it won't spring back well.

- Fancy pillow tops may feel plush initially, but they compress over time.

- Don't measure a mattress by its "ticking" or outer fabric design. You won't feel the fancy damask or silk when your sheet is covering it. But do check ticking for uneven stitching or broken threads. These are signs that the fabric could come loose and pucker.

- Manufacturers often give mattresses different names and make slight changes to the ticking just to make cost comparisons difficult. We suggest calling the manufacturer directly and asking if mattress A at one store is really any different from mattress B at another store.
- A nap test is the only real way to tell if a mattress is right for you. You'll feel silly doing it, but lie on the prospective mattress for at least ten minutes and in many positions. And definitely bring your partner along if you have one.
- Unless you know the exact name and model number of the mattress you want—and have tested it out in a store—we don't recommend buying a mattress by phone or online. Though there are some great deals to be had by going this route, the return policies are very limited. Most distributors offer an exchange only within a short trial period.
- We like shopping at stores with *comfort guarantees*. This means the store will let you exchange the mattress if you're not happy with it. But remember, when you buy from these stores, you could be purchasing a slightly used mattress someone has returned.
- Buy the mattress *and* the box spring, as they are meant to work together.

ORCHIDS

- Cheap doesn't mean bad. With orchids, you pay more for larger plants and for more exotic breeds.
- If this is your first experience with orchids, consider the low-maintenance phalaenopsis, or moth orchid. We're proud to report that we kept ours alive and healthy for months and months.
- A healthy orchid will have medium green, firm, unblemished leaves and no visible pests.

- Look for a plant that has at least a few unopened green buds. Light yellow prebuds that look slightly dried out will not flower.
- The container should be in proportion to the plant size. If it looks too small, be prepared to replant and factor in cost of a new container and additional mulch.
- Orchid bark mulch is better than moss because it provides better drainage. (Moss can keep roots wet for too long.)
- When shopping, be sure to ask if your orchid requires special care, as many varieties do.

FAST FACT: Vanilla beans come from the climbing orchid, *Vanilla panifolia.* The plant is native to Mexico, but 80 percent of the world's supply is now grown in Madagascar.

PICTURE FRAMES

- Avoid using untreated paper matting with any valuable artwork. The acid from the cellulose can leach into the art. Get acid-free paper instead. For really valuable stuff, get conservation framing.
- Consider UV-protected glass to protect the framed contents from fading, especially if you're framing a watercolor. Both UV-protected and nonglare glass cost about twice as much as regular glass.
- Oils and acrylics need to breathe and are rarely covered with glass. Watercolors and photos, on the other hand, are almost always covered with glass; just make sure it's raised from the surface of the art itself, or moisture can get in.

I prefer a collection of at least three frames of the same size and style over an eclectic mismatched look. Unless the frames are antique and the works are precious, I always go for the uniform appeal of a classic, simple frame.

–SARAH RICHARDSON, INTERIOR DESIGNER, FURNITURE DESIGNER, AND HOST OF *DESIGN INC.*

- Stay away from plastic frames—they scratch and warp with time. Aluminum is a better option. Wood is the most expensive, but offers the most timeless, traditional look.

ART

Art can be intimidating, no doubt about it. The best way to get comfortable with it is to get out there and start browsing the galleries, both big and small. In many galleries, a red dot beside a painting means the work has been sold. A blue dot means someone has expressed an interest, but you can still be added to the list. Don't focus on buying art as an investment. Buy it because it speaks to you in some way. Once you've made a choice, most galleries will allow you to take the work home on a trial basis. But before you plunk down the credit card, be sure to haggle. It's expected. Still can't afford it? You can always rent! If you do decide to buy, make sure the rental price is deducted from the sale price.

- A do-it-yourself framing place can save you 50 percent. But you may not have as wide a selection of frames as your custom frame shop.

PILLOWS

- Buy a pillow that fits your body. When you are lying on your side, the pillow should fully support the space between your shoulder and your head.
- Do not trust the SIDE SLEEPER or STOMACH SLEEPER labels on pillow packaging. These descriptions vary among manufacturers, so be sure to test the pillow out in the store. (This means lying down on a display bed, not on the floor—unless that's where you usually sleep, of course.)
- The fill and the fabric cover determine the price of the pillow. Down is most expensive; foam polyester is least expensive. And generally, the higher the thread count of the fabric cover, the more expensive the pillow.

BONUS BAG: Down pillows should be dry-cleaned once a year, while most synthetic pillows can be machine-washed. (Double-check the care label.) Using zippered pillow covers under your pillowcase will also protect your purchase.

- *Down blend* means there are feathers mixed in with the lighter, fluffier down. These pillows are heavier than the un-blended variety and can't be machine-washed.
- If you're buying a down-blend pillow, the fabric covering is key. (Poor-quality covers can let feathers poke through!) Look for a fabric cover with a minimum 200 thread count that has been well calendered. This means the fabric has been pressed between rollers to minimize any spaces be-tween the fibers.
- Goose down is considered the best feather fill. The higher the fill (500, 600, or 700), the firmer the pillow. (Refer to "Comforters and Duvets" on page 87 for more on this topic.)
- Down pillows make you sneeze? Consider a Primaloft fill. It's a polyester-based microfiber marketed as a down substitute and is often well priced.

PLANTS

- When shopping for houseplants, consider where you'll be placing them. Less than three hours of direct sun is consid-ered low light. Bright-light houseplants want as much light as possible—especially in the summer—and fare best near a south-facing window. Five hours of direct sun is considered high.
- Check the foliage. It should be shiny and green with new leaves that are a lighter green. Emerging foliage is a good sign.
- Make sure there are at least a few unopened buds on a flowering plant.
- Pull the plant out of the pot—yup, right in the store. If a lot of dirt falls away, it means the plant has been recently repotted into a larger pot, often just to be able to sell it at a higher price. It's usually cheaper to buy a big plant in a small pot and repot it yourself.
- If you are buying at a superstore like Home Depot or Wal-Mart, find out the delivery schedule for new plants, and shop that day for the best (and freshest) selection.
- Things to avoid include roots coming out the bottom of the pot, sickly looking leaves, pests, and anything slimy on the soil or on the pot.

FLOWERS

Buying flowers that are in season will get you the most volume for your money. When shopping, make sure the buds are slightly open. If they're too tightly closed, they may have been cut too early and might never open. With roses, squeeze the bud. If it's very soft, the flower is probably past its prime. We recommend buying something other than roses on Valentine's Day, when prices are often inflated up to 200 percent. And when ordering over the phone at any time, be sure to be clear about the price you want to pay *after* tax, delivery, or any other extra charges.

RUGS

- If decorating from scratch, start with the rug and work from there. Ask yourself, how much traffic will come through this room? Will it be used by kids? Pets? And how much furniture will cover it?

- When deciding on size, plan to leave about one foot between the carpet and the wall. Whether or not furniture should overlap the edge is a subject of much debate. (We say no!)

- Another size consideration—if choosing an area rug for a dining room, make sure the perimeter of the rug lies about three feet outside the table legs. When your guests pull their chairs out from the table, you don't want them to catch the edge of your new rug.

- Wool or silk rugs are typically the most expensive. The difference between them lies in their durability. Silk rugs are soft and luxurious. Wool rugs often have a denser pile, and they're more durable.

- Rugs made from acrylic have the appearance of wool. They won't last as long, but they come at a much lower cost. Rugs made from nylon or polypropylene are durable and soil resistant.

- Light-colored rugs tend to make a room look more spacious, but they obviously show off dirt.

- Take a paint chip or swatch of fabric with you to help match colors when shopping.

- A dealer or designer should let you take several options home so you can experiment. Some dealers will even do house calls and bring rugs with them, but there might be added pressure to buy.

- Beware of "liquidation," "going out of business" sales, and deep discounts in general. Regular prices have often been inflated so it appears you're getting a better deal.
- With oriental rugs, consider this: Patterns with a centerpiece or "medallion" work well in sitting areas where the furniture can be arranged around it. Patterns that emerge from corners or have a strong border look great in dining areas—where the table, not the carpet, is the focal point.

SOFAS

- For a long-lasting and sturdy sofa, go with a kiln-dried hardwood frame. The best woods are maple, poplar, ash, and oak. Avoid pine, particleboard, and plywood. They're not as strong as hardwoods.
- Ask about the joints. The ones that have been double doweled, screwed, and glued are the strongest.
- Pick up the sofa (or try to). A quality wood frame will feel heavy. If it feels lighter than it should, it could be made of plywood. Also, lift one corner. The other leg on that side of the couch should come up before the first leg is one inch off the floor. If it doesn't, the couch has a weak, flexible frame.
- Look for no-sag suspension—that's a zigzag spring that stretches from front to back. For even higher quality, go for eight-way hand-tied springs.
- With foam cushioning, we recommend a density rating of two pounds minimum. Sit on the sofa, and then get up. If you still see your impression, the foam density is too light.
- Foam encased in down fill feels extra soft and luxurious, but it's expensive and offers little support. Expect to continually plump up your cushions if you go this route.
- Upholstery is a big part of the price tag. A woven fabric is more durable than a printed one. If there's a pattern, make sure the design lines up along seams. Silk, linen, and wool are more fragile and more expensive than other fabrics.
- With leather, look for one that's aniline dyed. This means the dye goes all the way through the leather and won't show those bad scratches as much. (Though we feel a bit of wear makes leather look cozy and lived in.)
- We don't recommend buying a sofa from a catalog. Like mattresses, sofas need to be fully body-tested. Force your-

self to sit, lie, and lounge on the sofa for a good long while. This includes sitting on the armrests to check their sturdiness. Plan to do a lot of lounging with your sweetie? Then go shopping as a couple to make sure you both fit comfortably.

- Don't forget to check measurements to make sure the sofa will fit through the door. (Kristina learned this the hard way after the couch movers took big gouges out of the wall in an effort to get her new sofa down the stairs.)

TOWELS

- Look for towels with looped threads that are densely packed and tightly woven. More loops means better absorbency.
- Check the edges. They should be securely stitched to avoid fraying.
- Go for 100 percent cotton—it's the most absorbent material.
- "Egyptian cotton" refers to a type of cotton grown on trees that produce longer threads, *not* cotton grown in Egypt (though it can be). So "made in Egypt" doesn't guarantee that you are getting the real thing.
- Thicker towels have more material and therefore will absorb more water than thin towels. But they'll also take longer to dry.
- Velour is produced by slicing off the loopy surface of the fabric. It feels velvety and luxuriant to the touch, but the lack of loops means a lower absorbency. It also takes longer to dry than looped fabric.
- Don't pay full price for towels. They always go on sale.

SHOPPING BAGS VERDICT: We asked a bunch of strapping young water polo players to help us test towels. (We have such a hard job, don't we?) After mopping up with towels ranging in price from eight to eighty-five dollars, our testers proved to have somewhat expensive tastes. They found the fifty-eight dollar Italian-made towel with big loop threads to be the most absorbent.

4. Shock Value: Electronics and Appliances

Appliances aren't exactly sexy. But imagine a world without blenders (no more piña coladas), without hair dryers (frizz central), without espresso machines. (Kristina just had a heart attack.) And while some find navigating high-tech stores downright intimidating, many of us can't imagine going without a computer, let alone a television. So read on. Our A-to-Z buying guide is sure to take the shock value out of purchasing appliances and electronics.

ELECTRONICS

The electronics business is particularly competitive. And that means both good news and bad news for shoppers. The good news is that most stores sell similar goods at competitive prices. Retailers make money through volume.

While shopping around is always recommended, chances are you won't find huge price fluctuations from one big retailer to another. If you do chance on a good deal at one store, other shops will probably match it. If you find a flyer advertising a lower price elsewhere, take it with you and point it out. Or, ask the original store to write up a bill of sale so you can take the information with you to shop, compare, and ask for a price match.

Now the bad news. The markup on electronics is not that high. And that means there may not be much room to negotiate on the price. For example, when it comes to audio products (CD players, speakers, and the like) the markup is about 40 percent. For video products, like DVD players, the average markup is only 20 percent. This doesn't mean you shouldn't ask for a better deal; it may just require more sweet-talking.

Once you've made your purchasing decision, the salesperson will likely suggest you buy an extended warranty. As we mentioned in Commandment #8, "Stay on Your Game," we generally do not recommend purchasing these warranties, due to large profit margins of 70 to 100 percent! Extended warranties are a moneymaking business. Technology has come a long way, baby, and few products break down in their first year or two of life. The money you spend on the extended warranty usually goes directly to the salesperson's pocket and stays there. (One exception: the laptop or notebook computer. Since you're carrying it from here to there, the chances are greater it will get damaged, and an extended warranty might be useful.)

APPLIANCES

We give top marks to electronics retailers for making most products available to try right in the store, but the same cannot be said for many sellers of appliances. When shopping for a dishwasher, food processor, and the like, try to shop at stores that will allow you to turn on the machine before you commit. Listen for noise levels, and watch to see how much an appliance jiggles and moves. (We've seen blenders that dance across countertops.) Having completed rounds of appliance tests, trust us on this point: Loud, jittery appliances can really make time in the kitchen a headache-inducing chore. Don't forget to consider counter or cupboard space. Some appliances take up a lot of it.

Appliances and electronics are all about features. Heed Commandment #3, and Know What You Need. Write down on a piece of paper what you're shopping for, how you'll use it, who will use it, and how often. Reread that note while shopping, and it'll help you stay focused. A good way to save money on appliances or electronics is to buy refurbished, reconditioned, or remanufactured goods. These products have been sent back to the manufacturer for some reason and refitted with the appropriate parts. The manufacturer then approves the item for resale at a discount. Used can be a beautiful thing.

The reasons for refurbishment can vary. Sometimes it means that the product wasn't working and had to be fixed. It could just have a scratch on it that deterred potential buyers. Or perhaps it was simply returned by a customer and the box was opened. Most refurbished products do come with a new manufacturer's warranty. If you do go the refurbished route, we recommend going with big brand names, as these manufacturers are more likely to stand behind their products.

> While refurbished electronics may be a good deal, think twice before buying some floor models. That TV in the store may have been on for twenty-four hours a day, seven days a week for who knows how long.

Shopping for electronics and appliances doesn't end when you bring something home. Use the item right away to make sure it functions properly, lives up to the claims on its label, and does what you need it to do.

When it comes to buying appliances and electronics, we're plugged in.

HERE'S WHAT'S IN OUR SHOPPING BAG

BLENDERS

- A heavy base will help keep your blender stationary when it's turned on, and minimize turbulence!
- A shatterproof glass canister is worth the higher price. Glass adds to the weight of the machine and is more durable than plastic. Also, plastic canisters tend to retain food smells. A stainless-steel canister is good for keeping food cool, but you'll find it nearly impossible to keep tabs on the blending progress.
- Choose a canister with a narrow bottom and a long blade made of heavy steel. It will blend food effectively.
- A canister with measurement indicators is helpful if you do a lot of cooking.
- A blade that is permanently attached to the canister is harder to clean.

- You'll need at least 400 watts of power to crush ice easily. Higher-end blenders are usually around 600 watts.
- Three to five speeds are more than enough for most users. In fact, most professional blenders have an on-off switch and no speeds! So don't pay for too many bells and whistles you won't use.
- Check the buttons. Ones that are flush with the panel's surface are much easier to clean than protruding buttons.

CELLULAR PHONES

- Check out the size of the buttons and keypad. Some phones are so teensy tiny, the buttons can be difficult to manipulate, especially if you've got long nails.
- If you travel a lot, you'll need to buy a phone that has tri-mode capabilities in order to receive coverage in different countries and continents.
- Compare standby (the length of time your battery lasts without talking) and talk times of various phones.
- Scrolling is an important feature most of us use a lot. Experiment with it at the store to find which models are most convenient for you.

CELL PHONE PLANS

Remember, the devil's in the details. Going over your monthly plan by even thirty minutes can cost you big-time! Roughly calculate how many minutes you need a month, and then add another 10 or 15 percent. And do you make mostly local calls or national calls? Local plans are as much as 25 percent cheaper. Lastly, be sure compare the coverage area of different service providers to minimize costly roaming charges.

- We like flip phones. The phone is extra small when closed, but opens up to a more user-friendly size. The flip design also prevents you from making those unwanted calls that can happen when your phone gets crushed in a full handbag! This design is more delicate, though, so perhaps not the best choice if you have a young child who would be tempted to treat your phone as a toy.

COFFEEMAKERS

- Brewing temperature is critical to extract the flavors for a good cup of coffee, and should be around 200 degrees Fahrenheit. Look for a machine with a built-in thermometer, and if you discover the machine you bought doesn't get that hot, take it back for a refund.
- When shopping for a drip machine, look for one that has at least 1,000 watts of power.
- A thermal carafe will protect your freshly brewed java from oxygen—coffee's biggest enemy. This feature is especially useful if you plan on coming back for cup after cup.
- Consider capacity. If you make coffee only for yourself, there are machines that will brew coffee right into your travel mug. But if you're brewing for several people, look for a machine with a ten- to twelve-cup capacity (and remember that figure is based on five-ounce cups).
- Buy a machine with a cone-shaped filter rather than a flat-bottom filter. The *V* shape ensures that more water will come into contact with more coffee.
- Consider buying a pricier gold mesh filter that doesn't need the additional paper filter. It will last for years and reduces garbage!
- If you like your coffee served seconds after you stumble out of bed in the morning (don't even speak to Kristina before she's had hers), go for a machine that has a programmable timer so that you can set your cup of joe by your alarm clock. But if you're finicky about taste, this feature means your coffee grounds are exposed to the air throughout the night, causing them to lose flavor.
- We don't recommend buying a coffee machine with a water filter unless your tap water is bad. The water filter seriously jacks up the price.
- French presses are inexpensive and easy to store. But we found that the midpriced unit we tested produced weak coffee.

CORDLESS PHONES

- Look to see which radio frequency the phone uses to send the signal between the handset and the base. This will affect the price you pay. But a higher frequency doesn't necessarily mean a better phone, as they all experience some interference from other appliances (microwave oven, Internet link, and so forth) from time to time.

- Interference occurs when there are other appliances operating at the same frequency in the same room at the same time. If you're planning to put your phone in your kitchen, check the frequency of your microwave before you go shopping.

- *Spread Spectrum* is a feature you'll pay more for. It basically spreads your voice over multiple channels, so theoretically, it should reduce interference. But we've learned you can reduce or eliminate interference simply by moving the base to a new location.

- Models that sell extra handsets are a good choice for a busy household.

- Most of today's phones have a range sufficient enough to work throughout your house and yard.

- We like models that have a speakerphone option on the base. That way you can still answer the phone if you've temporarily misplaced the handset.

- Don't pay more for a phone with fancy gizmos like *voice enhancement.* We like the way we sound just fine!

- Illuminated buttons are a good feature if you tend to make calls late at night.

- If you hold the phone with your shoulder when you talk, avoid models with the TALK button on the back of the phone, as you'll keep hanging up on people by mistake.

DIGITAL CAMERAS

- Before you go shopping, ask yourself three questions: What will I use the camera for? Do I want to e-mail my photos? How much will I be enlarging photos?

- In addition to comparing prices of cameras themselves, you'll also need to compare costs of extras such as memory cards (the digital equivalent of film) in case you plan on taking many photos before you upload them to your computer.

- Resolution refers to the size of the photo in pixels. Generally, the higher the resolution, the better the printed photo will turn out. If you're publishing your pictures or making large prints, you'll want a higher resolution camera with five or six megapixels. If you're just e-mailing them to your friends, you'll be fine with two or three megapixels.

> I use a computer in my studio for layout now, and it's really valuable. But computer photography won't be photography as we know it—it [will] be something else. I think photography will always be chemical.
>
> **–ANNIE LEIBOVITZ,** **CELEBRITY PHOTOGRAPHER**

- Be sure to check out the quality of the lens. Some cheaper models of cameras have lenses made of plastic or poor grades of glass. Higher-end models have coated multilevel glass lenses.
- Look for a lens with an f-stop of 2.8. F-stop refers to the speed at which the aperture allows light to pass through the lens. An f-stop of 2.8 is a good setting for rookie photographers, as it allows more latitude for different light conditions.
- Digital cameras are dependent on batteries. Be sure to compare cost and shelf life of batteries from one camera to the next. You may also want to consider investing in rechargeable batteries. (See "Batteries" on page 210 for details.)
- If you like taking close-up shots of smaller subjects like flowers, bugs, and raindrops, you'll need to inquire about *macro focus* ability.
- Make sure the camera you buy is compatible with your home computer, and that you have the proper connection cables to upload the images from the camera to the computer.

DISHWASHERS

- Look for a dishwasher with the Energy Star designation. This means it meets strict energy-efficiency guidelines set by the U.S. Environmental Protection Agency and the U.S. Department of Energy. Because these dishwashers use less hot water than conventional models, you'll save about twenty-five dollars a year in energy costs.

- Make sure the dishwasher you're considering has two spray arms, and inquire about the pump. The better the pump, the stronger the water pressure, and that means your dishes get cleaner.
- Take your dishes shopping with you, and stack them inside to see how models compare. (Yes, we're serious.) Adjustable racks are a helpful feature, too.
- Check the quality of the rack. If you can make a dent with your fingernail, imagine what cutlery will do to it.
- A model that comes with three wash cycles—light, medium, and heavy—provides a lot of flexibility.
- Look for a model with an option to dry or not dry dishes. You can save a lot on energy costs by allowing the dishes to dry on their own.
- Examine the filter. The outer filter should be coarse enough to shield large food bits, while the inner filter should be fine so it can prevent smaller particles from getting through. Some filters need to be removed and cleaned manually.
- Don't pay extra for a *dirt sensor* feature. It doesn't necessarily clean dishes any better, uses more energy, and ups the overall price tag. Same goes for the *sanitizer* feature. As soon as you touch the dishes to put them away, they're no longer sanitized!
- The more places water can reach, the better the cleaning job. Multitiers or washer levels are a good design feature.
- If you can afford it, spring for a model with soundproofing. This way you can entertain your guests, watch TV, or chat with your dinner date without hearing that annoying noisy dishwasher in the background.

FAST FACT: Using a dishwasher can actually be more efficient than washing dishes by hand, assuming you use the dishwasher once for every three to four times you would wash the dishes yourself. Easier on your energy bill and on your cuticles!

DRYERS

- Check the dryer's electrical requirements. A machine that works on a 120-volt connection will take longer to dry clothes than one with a more powerful 220-volt connection (the same as the connection on your kitchen stove).

- Look for a model with moisture sensors and automatic shut-off to avoid overdrying clothes. This feature will save your favorite clothes and save you money on your electrical bill. But not all moisture sensors are created equal. The rod system (two rods that measure wetness when clothes fall across them) tends to be superior to systems that simply measure the temperature of the air in the dryer.

- A dryer with a large drum will do a better job of handling bulky items.

- A stainless-steel drum is extremely durable, but it will raise the price. Porcelain drums are economical but can sometimes chip when you throw in things with zippers.

- Look for a sturdy and wide lint filter. This will help prolong the life of your new dryer—so long as you clean it out after every load!

- Some energy-efficient dryers use low heat. They come with a higher initial price tag, but should save you money in the long run on your electrical bills.

- Check the types of ducts used. Metal ducts, like those made of aluminum, are safer and more durable than both plastic and foil. Plastic and foil can sag, and the lint can build up—creating a fire hazard.

- Dryers often have to fit into a specific space. Be sure to measure the dimensions before you go shopping.

BONUS BAG: It might sound crazy, but give your dryer a quick hit with the vacuum cleaner every six months—it's a great way to get rid of lint and help your dryer work more effectively.

ESPRESSO MACHINES

- In determining how much to spend on an espresso machine, factor in the amount you spend on coffee drinks outside the home. A three-dollar espresso, five days a week, adds up to $60 a month and $720 a year! You can get a great machine for half that amount. That said, be sure to factor in the cost of buying beans for your new machine, too, and know that you'll probably still buy the odd espresso from your favorite café every now and then!

- Machines that are purely steam driven are inexpensive, but they do not make real espresso. (The water has to be forced through the grounds to be considered the real thing.) This detail is often omitted on the box. Steam-driven machines are distinguished by a screw top for adding water.

- Traditional piston machines, which are distinguished by their brass or chrome finish and long lever, make excellent espresso, but they're expensive, take longer to warm up, and have a steeper learning curve. These machines are popular with espresso purists.

- The most popular type of espresso machine is the semiautomatic pump kind—and it's our favorite, too, because of the quality of the espresso it produces, the ease of use, and the price point. These machines will usually store water in a container at the back of the machine.

BONUS BAG: Top-of-the-line barbecues can't turn gristly meat into filet mignon. The same goes for high-end espresso machines and stale coffee beans. Our experts say the freshness of the coffee and the quality of the grind should be your first two considerations; the machine comes third.

- Less expensive semiautomatic pump machines typically last for seven to ten years, midprice machines ten or longer, and high-end machines twelve to fifteen years or longer.

- Ask if the machine has a three-way valve, a feature also found on commercial machines. It makes the machine less messy, and less temperamental, and extends the life of the machine.

- Super or fully automatic espresso machines are convenient, cleaner, and produce consistent espresso with the flip of a switch—all you add are the beans. They're great if you do a lot of entertaining and prefer to spend time with your guests, not with your espresso machine. But convenience comes at a cost. The price of these machines has come down in recent years as their popularity has increased, but they can still run as high as two thousand dollars.

- Good espresso is neither too watery nor bitter. It should be a reddish-brown color, which indicates it's been brewed at the right temperature and that the coffee is fresh. The espresso shouldn't drip or gush when it comes out, but pour out slowly, like honey or syrup. There should also be a layer of foam on the surface (also known as the *crema*), which helps retain heat and flavor. If your new machine doesn't produce espresso with these characteristics, take it back for a refund.

- Shop at a store or dealer that will provide follow-up service, as espresso machines tend to be temperamental and do require maintenance.

FOOD PROCESSORS

- Go for a model that can hold at least eleven cups (and that's a dry-cup measure). This will ensure the food processor you choose can do all sorts of different jobs.
- To test several brands of food processors, we cooked up a seemingly endless number of pizzas. The reason? Pizza making requires lots of different types of chopping and mixing, from the toppings to the cheese to the dough. We learned the most important food processor attachment by a long shot is the steel blade. We're willing to bet you wind up using it for 95 percent of your jobs.
- A direct-drive machine (where the motor sits under the bowl) will be heavier duty and more stable than a belt-driven food processor, where the motor sits off to the side. In our tests, we found that the latter tended to move across the countertop and couldn't handle the really tough jobs like making dough. Our advice? Invest in a direct-drive machine.
- Look for a machine that comes with a mini bowl as an attachment. It's really useful for those smaller jobs, like chopping garlic and mincing herbs.
- Make sure the feed tube is large enough to accommodate different sizes of food. The larger it is, the less prechopping you'll have to do. A large feed tube also makes it easier to add liquid ingredients while the machine is on.

FOOT SPAS

- The most important features to look for are moving water and a high-quality motor.
- Choose a foot spa with foot-operated controls. Foot controls make changing speeds and turning jets on and off super easy. But make sure the knobs and buttons are easy to manipulate with wet feet or hands.

- Don't bother with models that come with a remote control. Our testers found this feature was more hassle than it was worth.

- Foot spas with built-in massaging action may improve the overall experience, but they're harder to clean than a spa with a smooth bottom. Look for removable foot rollers for the best of both worlds.

- Pedicure attachments can be useful if you actually plan to give yourself a pedicure afterward. But if you're using a foot spa simply for relaxation purposes, you probably won't ever use them, so don't pay extra. We found we could easily do without.

- Consider the size of various foot spas. Have you got adequate storage space in your house?

- Make sure the foot spa you choose has good, strong handles so you can easily carry it while it's filled with water.

- A removable splash guard will help prevent a sloppy mess!

SHOPPING BAGS VERDICT: Who better to help us test foot spas than a pregnant dance instructor with very achy feet? After weeks of soaking our soles (yes, it's a hard job) we all agreed that the Dr. Scholl's foot spa was our favorite. It also makes a great Mother's Day gift.

GRILLS–INDOOR

- Examine the heating coils. They should be evenly spaced to ensure even heating and cooking.

- Variable temperature controls will allow you to cook a much broader range of foods at different temperatures. This is an important feature to look for, as many less expensive grills simply plug in and cook at a fixed temperature.

- Go for at least 1,200 watts of power, unless you're buying a double-sided grill. (The doubled-sided grills, like the George Foreman grill, don't need as much firepower, since they're cooking from both sides.)

SHOPPING BAGS VERDICT: We like double-sided grills for their speed and efficiency, and because you don't have to use cooking oils to get great grilling results. Anything that makes cooking easier and healthier gets top marks from us. (They're also great for making panini!)

- Any grill with lots of small spaces and ridges is going to be hard to clean. When you are cleaning, wipe the grill down while it's still warm. It'll make the job much easier than waiting till food has cooled and hardened.
- Look for thermostatically controlled indicator lights that will tell you when the grill has reached a desired temperature. This will take the guesswork out of your indoor grilling.

GRILLS–OUTDOOR (AKA BARBECUES)

- We prefer gas barbecues to charcoal barbecues because their cooking temperature is easier to control.
- Find out whether the barbecue you're considering comes with a gas tank. Some old tanks don't fit new grills. And will you have to put it together yourself? It might be worthwhile to pay a small fee and have the store do the assembly for you.
- If you're going with a charcoal grill, look for vents that will help you control the air flow as well as an adjustable grill that will allow you to cook food at various heights.
- With a gas barbecue, look at the number of BTU (British Thermal Units), which indicates heating power. The higher the BTUs, the hotter your barbecue can get.
- Other useful features for a gas barbecue include an outside thermometer, a shelf to warm plates or store food, individual controls for each element, and a gas-level gauge on the tank.
- Consider the grilling surface. Porcelain-covered wire is the most common and least expensive. Porcelain-covered cast iron retains heat well and does a good job of searing. Stainless steel is the easiest to clean and lasts a long time.
- Check out the wheels. Some barbecues come with four and a locking mechanism, while others come with two and need to be lifted. How often will you have to move it?
- If buying a portable grill, be sure to weigh it before you buy, especially if you plan to carry it a long distance on your camping trips.
- Shop for barbecues in the off season—especially the fall. You might have to wait until spring to use it, but you're more likely to get a deal.

HAIR DRYERS

- If you want to make the most of your curly hair, buy a hair dryer with a good-quality diffuser. It should be open and have spikes sticking out.
- Look for a *cold shot* button. The blast of cool air helps set the style of specific sections of hair and can close the hair cuticle.
- "Quiet" stylers are a great, considerate choice if you live with others.
- Be sure to buy a model with a removable filter. The ability to take it out and clean it periodically will add years to the life of your hair dryer.
- Test out the control panel at the store by holding the dryer in your typical drying position. Some designs have the control buttons in awkward places, causing you to change speeds and heat levels by mistake while styling.
- Higher wattage means higher heat. But don't go over 2,000 watts, or you could burn your hair or scalp.
- Look for a hair dryer with a long nose, which will allow you to direct heat more efficiently and keep long hair farther away from the filter, where it can get sucked in and burned.
- Thicker casing helps protect the motor and prevents cracks, even if you drop it.
- Check out the length of the cord, and make sure it's long enough for your setup at home.
- Professional hair dryers will cost more, but they do tend to dry hair faster (because of a stronger motor). But keep in mind they're heavier.

SHOPPING BAGS VERDICT: In our tests, the midpriced Vidal Sassoon dryer emerged as the favorite. It was light, quiet, and had multiple heat and airflow settings. The cheaper dryers we tested tended to be too noisy, while the top-of-the-line salon dryer was too heavy for our comfort—though it did dry hair the quickest.

HAIR-STRAIGHTENING IRONS

- Feel the weight of the iron. If it's too heavy, you'll get tired halfway through and not finish the straightening job. (Especially if you have a thick head of hair!)

- Choose an iron with ceramic-coated plates. While more expensive than other irons, they have more even heat distribution and glide over hair easily.
- Buy a product with multiple heat settings. Otherwise you'll always be straightening your hair on the hottest, most damaging temperature.
- We found some straightening irons took forever to heat up to the advertised temperature. Try to shop at a store where you can try a product before you buy. Or be sure to check it out as soon as you go home and take it back if it doesn't heat up quickly.
- Buyer beware: Many hairstyling appliances, including some straightening irons, claim to emit negative ions. These ions are supposed to react with the positive ions in the hair, closing the hair cuticle and thereby smoothing hair and reducing frizziness. However, we had a physicist test one negative-ion iron, and he found it didn't emit anything but heat. (To emit ions, you'd have to create a huge charge—something a small straightening iron can't possibly do.)
- Don't be fooled by "gold-plated" straightening irons. (Real gold is supposed to be a good heat conductor.) They are gold colored, maybe, but certainly don't contain any real gold.
- Look for straightening irons with smooth, rounded edges rather than sharp square ones that can give a crimped look.

FAST FACT: Thirty-five percent of women would rather have good hair days for the rest of their lives than great sex for the rest of their lives.

ICE CREAM MAKERS

- You'll pay less for a model that requires the canister to be prefrozen. This can take anywhere between six and twenty-four hours. We think it's best to store the canister in the freezer so it's always at the ready! And you'll also need to re-cool it if you want to make another batch.
- Consider what kind of ice cream—making experience you want. If you want convenience, speed, and homemade ice cream at the touch of a button, go for the full electric model. But if you prefer to roll up your sleeves and make it an event with your kids or dinner guests, choose an ice cream maker

that's more labor intensive (requiring you to stir, and so forth). The latter is also cheaper.

- Make sure the model you choose has no sharp corners or indentations where milk can get caught—such machines are difficult to clean. Sour milk—yuck!

- Look for thick plastic or metal churning paddles. They'll last longer than thin paddles.

- Manufacturers are often coming out with new versions, such as machines specifically for soft ice cream. But keep in mind that many such fad appliances are often discontinued, and it will be hard to get replacement parts if they break down.

IRONS

- We prefer irons with a bit of weight to them. They get the wrinkles out with less pressure than lightweight irons.
- Look for a temperature dial that tells you which fabrics should be ironed at which settings. It's like ironing "for dummies"!

- Buy an iron with a stainless-steel or a nonstick coated soleplate (like Durilium) for durability.
- Nonstick surfaces are easily scratched. Keep pins and zippers well away from these types of soleplates.
- Avoid Teflon—if you get something stuck on it, it's impossible to get off. Less expensive aluminum soleplates don't fare much better. They can corrode and become sticky over time.
- *Vertical steam* means the iron can produce steam when it's held upright. This is a handy feature to have if you own clothes made with delicate fabrics that dewrinkle best

SHOPPING BAGS VERDICT: Our tests found it's worthwhile to spend more for a good-quality iron. Paying less in this instance generally gets you an inferior product that you'll end up replacing more frequently. We say if you've got to spend time ironing, you might as well get the job done properly!

while hanging (like chiffon, silk, or velvet), or for ironing curtains while they hang on the rod.

- The more holes on the bottom of the iron, the more steam you'll have and the better pressed you'll be. (If you can't get much steam from your iron, trying ironing your clothes while they're still damp.)
- Look for a pivoting cord to avoid tangles. It also helps keep the cord from getting in your way while you work. If not a pivoting cord, then get one that's mounted in the center so it can be easily used by both left-handed and right-handed ironers.
- To avoid water dripping onto your clothes, look for an iron with an antidrip feature.

JUICERS

- There are two main types of electric juicers—centrifugal and masticating. Masticating juicers use pressure to squeeze out the juice. They work best with soft produce, like kale and bananas. They're generally more expensive than centrifugal machines and take longer to produce juice, but some models can double as food processors.
- Centrifugal juicers thrust produce against a rotating blade and then strain the juice from the pulp. This system produces more juice and is best used for hard produce, like carrots and apples.
- We like juicers with pulp ejectors. The pulp is expelled into a separate container, making cleanup easier. This feature is more common in centrifugal models.
- Wattage is important. Look for brands with as much horsepower as you can afford. If you can experiment with the juicer in the store, see if the engine warms up while it's juicing. If it heats up too much, you may lose enzymes in the process—a deal breaker for some juice purists.
- Choose a model with a large feed tube, and you'll have less chopping before juicing.
- Look for stainless-steel parts. They're durable and do a good job of retaining enzyme count.

KETTLES

- Stovetop kettles are cheaper and more reliable than electric models because they don't have any parts that can break down. But they do take longer to heat up and use up to 50 percent more energy than an electric model.

- With stovetop models, make sure the handle is far away from the spout. This will prevent a steam burn when pouring. Also make sure the grip is comfortable for you. Many kettles look fabulous, but they aren't easy to get a hold of—and if it's slightly uncomfortable now, imagine what it will feel like filled with water!
- Stovetop kettles with copper bottoms are pricey but energy efficient, as copper is a great heat conductor.
- With stainless-steel kettles, look for the 18/10 stamp on the bottom, referring to the chrome and nickel content. This combination is hard and fairly scratch resistant. (Note: this tip applies to any appliance or flatware made of stainless steel.)
- If you live in an area with hard water, consider an electric kettle with a flat plate element as opposed to one with a submerged element. It's easy to clean lime deposits off a flat surface.
- Look for an automatic shutoff on an electric kettle or a whistle on the stovetop type. Without it, you won't know when the water is boiling, and the kettle could boil dry.

LAPTOP COMPUTERS

- When it comes to big-ticket electronics like computers, we like to go with well-known name brands like Apple and Compaq. You're likely to find a local big-name dealer nearby if you need something repaired, and the bigger brands constantly compete to provide the best technical support.
- Budget-priced laptops will work for simple word processing and e-mail, but they'll have slower processors, small screens, and less memory (which is measured in RAM). Higher-end models will have more RAM, faster processors, and larger, better-quality screens.
- Generally speaking, if you can afford to spend more on anything, spend it on more RAM and a faster processor. These two components will make your computer faster, more versatile, and give you an overall stronger machine. (Note: manufacturers like Intel [Pentium] are constantly coming out with new versions of their processors, so you'll need to read up on what's out there before you buy.)
- Screens can come as small as twelve inches and run as large as seventeen inches. Bigger screens will weigh more—and cost you more—but if you expect to use your laptop for watching movies or playing games, it's money well spent.

- Lithium ion batteries are the best-quality batteries around and are becoming standard issue with new laptops. Find one that promises at least three hours of battery life.
- Play with the keyboard to get a feel for the keys. Some small laptops may feel cramped.
- If you don't like the onboard mouse, attach an external one. It's a small price to pay for greater ease of use.
- Consider weight. Some models weigh only three pounds and are ultraslim and light. But note, they tend to skimp on speed to save battery power. That's good for frequent flyers, but not so great for more stationary users. And if you go too light, you'll often have to give up other features, like larger screens.
- If you plan to travel with your laptop a lot, consider an extended warranty, especially for the screen. (This is one instance where we think an extended warranty is a good idea—see Shopping Commandment #8, "Stay on Your Game" on page 10 for more on this topic.)

MICROSTEREOS

- Microstereos are a good option for technophobes. Everything comes in one unit (the amplifier, receiver, CD player, and so on) except for the speakers. It's basically plug in and play!
- Don't buy a microstereo based on the wattage. High-quality speakers don't need tons of power to sound good. Microsystems are designed for small rooms, and most have more than enough power to fill those rooms with sound.
- Bring your own music to the store with you when shopping—you know how your favorite tunes are supposed to sound.
- Don't test speakers through headphones unless you plan

> Don't focus on wattage. Look at the accessibility of the controls, how easy they are to use, the easy in-out of the CD, the volume. Look for treble, mid, bass controls with numbers so they can be set to zero or the same for each listen.
>
> **–RANDY BACHMAN,** MULTIPLATINUM SINGER-SONGWRITER

to always listen that way—you won't get an accurate sense of how they sound.

- Not all systems can play MP3 files, so if you plan to burn your own CDs, check that the system can handle it, especially if you're buying an older model or something second-hand.

- You can upgrade your microstereo speakers, but don't go too big—the unit may not have enough power to support them.

- Paying more may get you a sleeker design, but it doesn't guarantee a better sound. We blared four systems from behind a black curtain and asked singer-songwriter Randy Bachman to help us pick a favorite. We found that inexpensive systems sounded just as good as or even better than units that costs two or three times as much.

MICROWAVES

- The more watts a microwave has, the faster it cooks. Microwaves smaller than one cubic foot typically have 800 watts, while larger machines have 1,000 or 1,100. How many watts you need depends on how you'll be using it and how much space you have.

- Look for one with a turntable—it heats and defrosts food most evenly.

- Buy the biggest microwave that can fit in your kitchen. If you're short on space, look for over-the-range or under-the-counter models.

- A convection microwave can double as a regular oven. But they are more expensive and larger than regular microwaves.

- If you're planning only to reheat meals and warm up liquids, then you don't need sensor cooking and other programming options. That said, we think the following features are worth paying for: defrost buttons, power-level options, one-touch time buttons (one minute, two minutes, and so forth), and child safety locks.

MP3 PLAYERS—PORTABLE

- If you're looking for an MP3 player to accompany you on a treadmill or in the car, a flash-memory player is a good choice. These players can be the size of a pen or a matchbook, and they don't have moving parts, so skipping is eliminated. Drawbacks? Their super light weight and small size makes them easier to lose than larger models, and most can hold only about two hours of CD-quality music (slightly more if you use lower-quality audio files).

- Hard-core audiophiles who want thousands of songs at their fingertips should opt for a hard-disk player (like Apple's ever-popular iPod). These players are often bulkier than the flash-memory kind. They can also have a shorter "live" time because they pack so much more memory.
- If you're shopping for a hard-disk player, look for one with skip protection. This means upcoming songs on the playlist are stored in a memory buffer, which minimizes and prevents songs from jarring when you're on the move.
- Generally, the more memory, the better. But added memory will cost you.
- Battery life depends entirely on the player and the settings used. That said, flash-memory players tend to be easier on batteries than hard-disk players, and they run on easily replaceable alkaline batteries or rechargeables. Hard-disk players usually come with a rechargeable nonremovable battery, which can be expensive to replace after the warranty period.
- We like units with auto shutoff—they power down after being left unused to save battery life.
- Whatever player you choose, make sure it's compatible with your computer. You'll also need a FireWire or USB port to transfer the audio files you download to the player. If you have an older computer, make sure you know its specs and the operating system version before heading to the store.

PERSONAL DIGITAL ASSISTANTS (PDAs)

- The major choice is between models that use the Palm Operating System (OS) and Microsoft's PocketPC system.
- Palm OS–based PDAs use special software that's compatible with Windows or Mac programs, depending on the unit you choose. If you're just looking for the basics, these types of PDAs are the easiest to use.
- PocketPCs are for more advanced users who plan to fully incorporate the PDA into their workday. The units tend to have more powerful processors and are designed to be like mini-

computers, coming with stripped-down versions of Windows, Internet Explorer, and multimedia software like MP3 players.

- The more memory space a model comes with, the more software it can handle. Most PDAs come with enough memory for the average user, but if you expect to use many different programs, make sure the model you're considering has an expansion slot for adding a memory card. (Most new models have at least one.)

- If you want your PDA to connect to the Internet using a wireless connection, you'll need to buy a Wi-Fi networking card that fits into an expansion slot on the PDA.

- The latest PDAs are powered by rechargeable lithium ion batteries. Battery life varies between five hours of continuous use to twenty hours or more, so compare units at the store. That said, take any manufacturer estimates with a grain of salt, as live time really depends on how much you use the PDA.

- PDAs with replaceable alkaline batteries are usually less expensive than ones with rechargeable batteries, but we found they ate through batteries quickly. Factor that cost into the initial price.

- Some models come with built-in cell phones, digital cameras, and wireless connectivity. Impressive but expensive. If you experience features-and-sales-pitch-overload at the store, recall Shopping Commandments #3, Know What You Need, and #8, Stay on Your Game!

REFRIGERATORS

- All refrigerators work basically the same way. Spending more will get you a quieter compressor muffled by thicker insulation and more cosmetic features—like a computerized shopping list, a stainless-steel front, or a fancy door that matches your cabinets.

- There are three basic configurations to choose from: side-by-side, freezer-on-top, or freezer-on-bottom. We like the freezer-on-bottom configuration best because you get to browse for food at eye level, rather than bending over as you have to do with the freezer-on-top design (unless, of course, you really need to have your Ben & Jerry's at eye level).

- Side-by-side refrigerators often come with extra features like ice machines, but they're usually more expensive than other configurations. We've also found that freezers with this configuration don't fit as many odd shaped items (like pizza boxes).

- Refrigerators are the single biggest energy consumer in most households. If you're buying a new fridge, look for an energy card that will show you how much energy your new appliance will use, and look for the Energy Star sticker. Replacing a fridge purchased in 1990 with a more recent Energy Star–qualified model will save enough energy to light the average household for five months! (And save you a lot of money on your electric bill.)

- You'll need sixteen to twenty cubic feet for two people. Add an extra foot for every person.

- Glass shelves are sturdy and easy to clean, but they do show spills more easily. If you go for a fridge with wire shelves, look for a heavy gauge, and make sure the wires are close together and have center support.

- Stainless steel looks great, but it shows fingerprints, scratches easily, and can be hard to keep clean—especially if you have little kids running around.

- While handy, ice makers are notorious for breaking down and can be a costly repair. (Kristina knows from experience!) If you just can't do without your ten pounds of ice a day, make sure the warranty covers ice-maker repairs.

SEWING MACHINES

- Before you buy, you need to decide how much sewing you're going to do. The occasional or novice sewer will do well with a mechanical model. A devoted or experienced sewer may want a more costly computerized machine.

- Big-chain department stores tend to offer basic models. For a higher-end model, and for those who need help getting started, we recommend shopping at a specialty store.

- If you decide to go with a computerized model, find out what software the machine comes with. A basic package will have simple patterns, but additional, more complicated software patterns will add to the cost.

- Test-drive the machine before buying. Bring a variety of materials to the store, and sew on each one—using several different stitches—to get a feel for the machine.

- A good, basic machine should be easy to thread-feed fabric through evenly, be able to take multiple layers of fabric, and produce even and tight stitches. It should also have variable speeds, create clean buttonholes, have a decent-size foot pedal, feel sturdy, and sew smoothly without vibrating.

- Lift a portable machine to see if you can carry it easily.
- Spending more doesn't always get you more. In our tests, we found that a higher-end mechanical machine had a much clunkier sew than a model that was hundreds of dollars cheaper.
- Looking for a bargain? Buy in the summer months when sales are at their annual low and suppliers reduce their prices to distributors. Also consider visiting craft shows to spot manufacturer deals.
- For the warranty to be valid, the vendor must be an authorized dealer.
- If you're buying used, know that a warranty technically expires when the machine changes hands. That said, a reputable retailer will indeed honor the warranty if the previous owner has kept the original receipt. Check this out before buying.

TELEVISIONS

- Screen size is measured diagonally. Aspect ratio is the ratio of the width to the height. Most basic TVs are 4:3; widescreen TVs are 16:9.
- Bigger is not always better. If you're going to sit less than ten feet away, a twenty-seven or a thirty-two inch should do it.
- Pick your TV depending on the viewing area. Conventional or direct-view TVs work best in bright rooms. But the curved screen means you'll get some distortion when viewed from the sides.
- Flat-screen TVs take up less space than conventional models, and they have less distortion and glare.
- If you want a really big picture, go with a rear-projection TV. They're great for watching sports but are not without their drawbacks. Notably, they require lots of space, you need to frequently fiddle with and align the CRTs (cathode ray tubes), and if you sit too close, you'll see lines. Plus the image gets darker or dimmer when viewed from different areas in the room.
- Want to sit up close? LCD screens (like your computer monitor) provide the best small picture.

- Pick a TV depending on what you watch. If you watch regular TV (analog) and VHS tapes, a conventional TV is fine. High-definition TVs will shine only if you watch digital networks, receive your signal from satellites, or play lots of DVDs. (The same is true of plasma screens.) That said, a high-definition TV does provide the clearest picture possible.

BONUS BAG: So when is it time to get a new TV? Here's a good guideline: If your TV is no longer under warranty and it's going to cost half the value of a new one to repair it, it's time to go shopping.

- HD-ready or HD-capable sets require an external receiver/decoder for viewing HD signals. Integrated HDTVs are ready to go.
- Plasma screens are the best of the best. They provide a wider viewing area than LCD screens and have amazing picture quality. But be prepared to pay for it, and keep in mind that plasma sets consume more power than any other type of television. They also need proper ventilation because they give off so much heat.
- If you plan to hook up a sound system, check to make sure the model has audio/video outputs and an audio input. DVD players and cameras need an S-video input.
- As with any electronic product, you pay more for features like *picture in picture*. Ask yourself how often you'll really watch two shows at once.

TOASTERS

- The first thing to keep in mind when shopping for a toaster: You're only making toast! Some toasters come with liquid crystal displays (LCDs) and microchips. In our tests, none of these fancy features made a difference in the quality of toast.
- Check the shade selector. Do you really need to be able to make toast in one hundred shades, or will light, medium, and dark work just as well?
- Don't pay more for a defrost button. Regular toasting can easily defrost frozen bread.

- Look down the toaster slots, and check out the nichrome wires—those are the ones that heat up. Closely laid wires will provide more even toasting. Need toast fast? (And who doesn't, really?) Units with more than 1,000 watts of power make for a shorter toasting time.
- Check the timing mechanism. Mechanical toasters turn off when a small wire heats up and bends to a certain angle. With multiple toasting, the wire is already warm, so it bends more quickly. That makes the first piece of toast darker than the subsequent pieces. We prefer electronic models because they are more consistent.
- Can't tell if it's mechanical or electronic? Press down on the lever on an unplugged machine. If it stays down, it's mechanical.
- Look for a model with slots wide enough for bagels and waffles.
- Cool-touch housing keeps the outside of the toaster cool to prevent little fingers from getting burned.
- Most toasters come with an automatic shutoff if the toast gets jammed. But in our tests, only one toaster turned off before it started smoking, even though they were all tested by Underwriters Laboratories, an internationally recognized safety tester. Our advice—don't rely on shutoff systems and *don't* leave toasting bread unattended.

FAST FACT: Though invented in 1909, the toaster didn't really take off until the advent of sliced Wonder bread in the 1930s.

VACUUMS

- The style of vacuum that's best for you depends on the ratio of carpet to bare floor in your home.
- Uprights have their weight in the base and a hefty rotating brush that loosens and sucks dirt as you push back and forth. Their heavy suction makes them great on carpets, but look for a unit that allows you to turn off the brush so you can use it on uncarpeted floors.
- Canisters are best for homes that have more bare floors than carpet, and are handy in hard-to-vacuum places like stairs.

- Don't worry about the number of amps. Amperage refers only to the amount of electrical current, not to the suction power.
- We don't recommend paying more for HEPA (High Efficiency Particulate Air) filters that are supposed to stop fine, allergy-inducing particles from escaping. Many non-HEPA vacuums do this job just as well.
- Things like *dirt sensors* are fancy features that just jack up the price, and we found they didn't make a big impact on overall performance.
- Look for a cog belt versus a flat belt. Cog belts are more reliable.
- Bagless vacuums sound like a good idea, but you still have to empty them *and* clean them out regularly. We prefer machines with bags that will hold the dust and other vacuumed contents. And look for vacuums that have a full-bag indicator, which tells you when the bag needs to be changed—it really takes the guesswork out of this less-than-pleasant household chore.
- Turn the machine on in the store. A good vacuum will operate quietly.

HAND VACUUMS

Small hand vacuums are handy, especially if you live with a lot of messy Marvins. While corded models have limited reach, they tend to be more powerful and more affordable. If you have pets, choose a hand vacuum with a rotating head, also known as the *beater bar*. It's good at picking up fur and hair. And take a pass on wet vacs. They require a lot of extra maintenance, as you have to empty that spilled milk ASAP. We recommend sticking to paper towels for those wet cleanups.

VIDEO CAMERAS

- We recommend going with a digital camera versus an analog one, especially if you plan to do any editing on your home computer. Digital cameras are also lighter, which makes shooting for long periods of time altogether easier. All the better to take to your kids' dance recital!
- There are three types of digital video cameras: MiniDV, Digital 8, and DVD. MiniDVs are the most popular type and are a

good choice if you want high-quality video images; Digital 8s are lower in price and aren't as widely available; a DVD camera will allow you to record in the same format as commercial DVDs.

- Cameras with large liquid crystal display (LCD) viewing screens are cool to use, but viewing or shooting through the screen, as opposed to the eyepiece, is a big drain on batteries.

- A charge-coupled device (CCD) converts light into pixels. The higher the number of pixels, the sharper the picture. (Most cameras have 250,000 pixels or more.) Pricier cameras have more than one CCD to better filter light levels.

- The smaller and lighter the camera, the harder it will be to hold steady. Look for models with an electronic or optical image stabilizer. Viewers of your home movies will thank you.

- We recommend shopping at a store that gives you easy access to cameras so you can test them out. If they don't have them out on display, make sure the salesperson takes the camera out of the box so you can play with it.

- Don't pay more for a video camera that also produces stills. In our experience, the quality of the stills is not great, so it's better to buy your still-photo camera separately.

BONUS BAG: A note about DVD video camera discs: DVD-RAM discs are reusable but aren't compatible with all DVD players. DVD-R and DVDTR discs work with most DVD players but can be used only once. Factor these costs into your budget, and make sure you know the DVD player's specs before you head to the store.

WASHING MACHINES

- Look for a washer with the Energy Star designation. This means it meets strict energy efficiency guidelines set by the U.S. Environmental Protection Agency and the Department of Energy and uses 50 percent less energy than a standard washer.

- Ask if the machine has a direct-drive or a belt-driven transmission. Direct drive will need fewer repairs but have a bigger price tag.

- Front loaders are more expensive to purchase but cheaper

to operate. Top loaders are cheaper to buy and cheaper to fix, but they use more water and therefore cost more to run.

- Most front loaders have 25 percent more capacity than top loaders. This is because top loaders have a space-hogging agitator in the center of the drum.
- Electric controls are more difficult to fix than mechanical dials.
- When analyzing settings, remember that most people require only a two-speed wash cycle (regular and delicate wash), a spin cycle, water level controls, and three temperature settings. The rest is gravy.

SHOPPING BAGS VERDICT: We tested four washing machines—two top loaders and two front loaders—to see which one could get a load of super muddy white shirts the cleanest. It was a total wash! We couldn't see any difference among them—they all came out fairly clean. But we still like front loaders best because they are gentler on our clothes. And if you're going to spend money on fancy duds, we say take care of them!

5. Who's Hungry?: Food and Libations

Today's grocery stores are increasingly labyrinthine, with hundreds of new products appearing every year. Trendy diets are adding to the confusion as low-fat, low-carb, lite, and light products crowd the shelves. The question is, What are the tastiest, healthiest, and most cost-effective products for you and your family?

But the grocery store is just one stop along your way to a well-stocked pantry. Of course, in many states you'll also need to visit the liquor store to complete the menu for all those fabulous dinner parties you throw (and perhaps to take the edge off after a hard day of sale shopping!). The following pages will reveal all the tips you need to make the right purchase, whether you're buying a pound of butter or a magnum of chardonnay.

FIRST STOP, THE GROCERY STORE

Pay close attention to the labels. Labeling laws fall under the jurisdiction of the Food and Drug Administration. If you know how to decipher a label, you can be discerning about what makes it into your cart.

> When it comes to supermarket flyers, remember this: The best sales are found on the front and back cover. So if you don't have time to flip through it all, just scan the front the way you would your morning newspaper.

Light. A product labeled *light* contains at least one-third fewer calories or half the fat of its regular counterpart. This means "light" products from two different brands can contain drastically different amounts of fat or calories (or both), so you'll need to compare them. *Light* can also mean the salt content of the product has been cut by 50 percent. But read carefully—*light* can also be used to describe things like texture and color (like *light and moist* on a cake box). The intent of the word just has to be clear in that latter case.

"High" or "Good Source Of." Lots of food labels have statements claiming to be a good source of iron or some other nutrient. But in order to display the words *good source of,* the product must contain at least 10 percent of a nutrient's recommended daily intake (described on the label as *Daily Value*). To claim that a product is *high* in some nutritional value, it must contain at least 20 percent of the recommended daily intake.

Organic. Manufacturers or farmers that sell more than five thousand dollars a year in organic products have to be certified by the U.S. Department of Agriculture in order to put the word *organic* anywhere on their product. Simple enough, but *where* the word appears on the label indicates what percentage of the ingredients are certified organic. This can get complicated. Here's the rundown: *100 percent organic* means all of the product's ingredients are certified organic; *organic* means 95 percent or more of them are; while products that describe ingredients as organic anywhere prominently on the front of the package (*with organic raisins, dates, and millet*) are 70 percent certified organic.

More often than not, pricier brand-name products occupy eye-level shelves—the prime real estate. Check out upper and lower shelves for less expensive or generic brands.

Be aware of product placement. One of Anna's biggest shopping challenges is to get in and out of the grocery store with nothing more than what is on her list! Watch for tactics like the following:

Product Pairings. That's the salad dressing beside the lettuce or the chocolate sauce on a stand right next to the ice cream. Suddenly you're envisioning diving into a bowl of ice cream with chocolate sauce when all you came for was the ice cream (more money out the door *and* more calories!). Seeing such food items suggestively placed side by side may make you add extra items to your basket, especially if you shop while hungry.

"Special" Bins. They're often located at the end of aisles and contain products that have been pulled away from their usual shelfmates. You may find toilet paper at the end of the cereal aisle, for example. The idea here is to draw your attention to a product that looks like a deal. But be clear, *special* does not necessarily mean "on sale." Most often, the store has simply overstocked the product. Compare the bin prices with the shelf prices.

Dominant Brands. Ever notice the array of choices for something as simple as microwave popcorn? There's regular, butter flavor, reduced fat, organic—even smoked! The more choices there are of one brand, the more shelf space it takes up, and the more likely you may be to buy from that particular company. Manufacturers often design their packages with the exact dimensions of shelves and freezers in mind.

> Grocery stores are strategically organized. The essentials like milk, produce, and meat are placed around the edges and back of the store, forcing you to pass other tempting products as you walk through. And it's no mistake that the bakery department is near the front either. Smell that fresh bread!

Convenience foods. Items like premade meals can save you time. Whether they're worth the typically huge price increase depends on your needs and the item itself. For the most part, we like buying prewashed lettuce, even though a head of lettuce goes for ninety cents and a bag costs around four dollars. It saves time, hassle, and mess, and makes it easier to eat our veggies. We try to stay away from microwave popcorn (all those additives and hydrogenated oils!) and products in squeeze bottles (they're often more expensive, and is it really that hard to get mayo out of the jar?). The bottom line—compare the cost and added fat, calories, or salt with the regular item, and weigh whether the convenience is worth it.

NEXT STOP, THE LIQUOR STORE

Having a little wine with dinner or preparing for a big shindig? You have to have your wits about you when buying alcoholic beverages, so don't lower your guard just yet.

It may sound strange but alcoholic beverages and real estate have one thing in common—it's all about location, location, location! You can learn a lot about a wine or spirit based on where it's from. Getting a handle on Scotland's geography will help you pick a great scotch. And new-world wines generally taste heavier than old-world wines, which tend to be more complex. But when it comes to beer, watch out for undercover imports! If you've enjoyed a bottle of Japan's Kirin in North America, chances are it came from the company's plant in Los Angeles. For more specifics, refer to our entries on buying beer, champagne, gin, scotch, vodka, and wine in this chapter.

The shape of the wine bottle is another thing to take note of, and it can give you clues to taste and region of origin. A sweet white usually comes in a flute-shaped bottle; dry reds and whites come in Bordeaux bottles; and chardonnays and pinot noirs come in bottles with big bottoms. The reason for the different bottle shapes is just simple tradition, with one notable exception. Champagne bottles demand thicker glass, soft sloping shoulders, and a deeper punt in the base because the pressure in the bottle is so much higher than for still alcohols.

While you're browsing the liquor store (as we like to do), keep a close eye on those little ratings cards that are often posted on the shelves. Look for third-party reviews, such as those written by magazines like *Wine Spectator* or by Robert Parker, a respected wine expert. Just make sure the vintage referred to in the rating is the same as the one on the bottle. (They're often different!) Some reviews are written by the beverage producers themselves, and we take those with a grain of salt. And if we find a bottle we like, we always inquire about buying it by the case. Some wineries and retailers offer discounts to customers who buy in bulk—sometimes as high as 20 percent. It never hurts to ask.

And if you find the prospect of ordering wine at a restaurant daunting, try this: Peruse the wine list for something that stands out, perhaps a single bottle listed under a country not known for its wine (a cabernet from Turkey, for example). Chances are it's a treasure uncovered by the restaurant's sommelier and worth a taste.

———

The following are some common purchases at the grocery store and the liquor store. We've shopped for and tested these items ourselves to uncover the tastiest shopping tips. Hope you're hungry!

HERE'S WHAT'S IN OUR SHOPPING BAG

BALSAMIC VINEGAR

- True balsamic comes from either Modena or Reggio Emilia, Italy. If one of those names isn't on the label, the product is an imitation.
- There are two types of balsamic vinegar: *tradizionale* and commercial/industrial.
- *Tradizionale* represents only a small portion of the market. To be called a true *tradizionale*, the balsamic must have been deemed so by a consortium of experts. *Tradizionale* is typically bottled into a distinctive small bottle, bears an official seal of approval, and can cost hundreds of dollars. It is thick, rich, and a perfect balance of sweet and sour—delicious poured over ice cream!
- Commercial/industrial balsamic costs far less than *tradizionale,* and there is a great deal of variety when it comes to flavor and quality.
- If the age is printed on the label, keep in mind it is a blend of several years and that the age on the bottle represents the oldest age. The older the balsamic, the better.
- Bad imitations abound! A balsamic vinegar wannabe is often simply red wine vinegar cut with water with caramel or sugar added. The label should clearly identify the use of *grape must* or *balsamic* as an ingredient.

- Swish the vinegar around in the bottle. A good balsamic will have "legs" that coat the inside, as a syrup would.

BEER

- Lager is lighter and crisper than ale or stout. (Germany and the Czech Republic are known for making good lagers.) Pilsner is a type of lager hailing from the Czech Republic and has a slight hoppy flavor.
- Ales tend to be fruity, floral, and spicy. (Some drinkers may also find them sweet.) They're more full-bodied than lagers. Many good ones come from the UK. Cream ale is light to medium-bodied. India pale ale is high in hops (which helped preserve it on sea journeys). It tends to be a bit bitter and goes well with spicy foods. (We love it with Thai dishes!)
- Porter has a dark, toasted, and sometimes slightly chocolatey flavor and goes well with rich flavors, like smoky cheeses and red meat.
- Stout is the darkest beer. It's very full-bodied and is made from roasted barley.
- Buying Belgian beer is a safe bet, as Belgium is considered to be one of the best beer producers in the world—it produces more than eight hundred varieties.
- Some critics say unpasteurized beer has the best flavor. Microbrews are usually unpasteurized.
- Beware of the term *no preservatives*—hops are natural preservatives and don't need extra additives to stay fresh.
- Some producers add grains other than malted barley, like rice or corn grits (a cheap starch), to their beer. Experts say beer made only with barley may cost more but has a stronger flavor.
- The color of the glass bottle can make a difference in the beer's taste. Clear or green glass allows light to come through and can give beer a musky taste over time if exposed to the light. Brown glass is preferable.

BONUS BAG: When planning a dinner party or barbecue, follow this general rule: Foods that you pair with white wine will also work with lagers. Red wine–friendly foods work with ales.

- A darker color of beer is not necessarily an indicator of a heavier flavor. Darker beers will taste more toasty.

BOTTLED WATER

- The source of the water should be printed on the label, as this can indicate taste, mineral content, and how the water is processed.

- Springwater comes from an underground water source that has flowed naturally to the surface, and it's bottled at the site. Glacier water is handled and bottled in a similar way. Both types tend to have a higher mineral content than other waters, which gives them a slight flavor.

BONUS BAG: Even the best mineral waters don't pack as many minerals as your basic carrot stick. So don't buy bottled water for the minerals; buy it for the hydration!

- Choose mineral water if you want springwater with a higher, naturally occurring mineral salt content and a more distinct flavor. Some bottling companies add carbon dioxide to protect freshness. Under FDA regulations, their natural mineral content can't be modified by any other chemicals.

- Looking for less flavor and a flatter taste? Buy demineralized water, purified water (drinking water that has been additionally treated using filtration or ozonation), or distilled water (drinking water purified using a heating process).

- While some bottled waters have a best-before date, most experts say it's more of a taste-assurance date than anything else. Bottled water doesn't "go bad," per se; it can just acquire a plasticky aftertaste over time—especially if it's been stored in a hot place, like on a windowsill or in a car. Keep it somewhere cool and away from direct sunlight.

- Look for an NSF stamp on the label. That means the product has been inspected by a third party and has met the certification standards set by the FDA.

- Read the ingredients. Some waters have added sodium—not good for those on restricted diets. (Though water with added sodium was the favorite among our taste testers.)

- When traveling, remember that some countries aren't as strict with water regulations (though other countries will, in fact, be stricter than the U.S.). It's safer to stick to brand names you trust, or carbonated waters, which are treated during the carbonation process.

BUTTER AND MARGARINE

- Both butter and margarine have the same amount of fat and roughly the same number of calories (36 calories per teaspoon). The big difference is that butter is an animal product and contains cholesterol, while margarine is plant-based and therefore cholesterol free. But whether one is healthier for you than the other is up for debate.
- Butter is a natural product with only salt added. It is produced by separating the cream from the milk and then churning it until it thickens. To be labeled butter, a product must contain at least 80 percent milk fat by weight. (Something labeled *European butter* probably has more milk fat.)
- Butter also contains more saturated fat than margarine, which is why it is not recommended for people on heart-healthy diets.
- Margarine is usually made with vegetable oil (olive or canola oils are best), and may also contain water and preservatives. If a product is labeled *margarine,* it must contain 80 percent fat by weight.
- Reduced-calorie margarine has less fat and fewer calories because more water has been added. This type of margarine is not good for use in baking and cooking.
- Whipped butter is just regular butter with air or inert gas mixed in. This is our first choice because it's less dense and therefore has fewer fat and calories, but still has all the taste.
- Some products advertise being fortified with vitamins or calcium. But these ingredients are usually added

SHOPPING BAGS VERDICT: Our blind-taste-test testers preferred the taste of butter to margarine when it was served on bread—especially the organic and whipped butters. But in our chocolate chip cookie test, the margarine cookies were the overwhelming favorite. Grandma would be floored!

in such small amounts, they won't do much to improve your health.

- Don't be sucked in by the words *cholesterol free* on a margarine label. All margarine is cholesterol free because it's plant-based.
- Some margarines contain trans fats—said to increase bad cholesterol levels in the body while decreasing good cholesterol levels. Solid stick margarines are the worst trans fat culprits. Instead, choose soft nonhydrogenated margarines that come in tub containers.

CAT FOOD

- Most, but not all, commercial cat foods are formulated to the standards set by the American Association of Feed Control Officials (AAFCO). These guidelines offer the *minimum* requirements necessary for a cat's nutritional health, so look for statements on the package that indicate it "meets or exceeds the guidelines set forth by the AAFCO" to ensure the food is nutritionally complete.
- Cats digest carbohydrates like other mammals, but their digestion improves with more finely ground food.
- Buy cat food that will give your cat a diet that consists of around 30 percent protein and 8 percent fat every day based on a 4,000 kilocalories per kilograms of dry matter diet. This daily intake can be reached using dry food, wet food, or a combination of the two.
- Look for FEEDING TRIAL on the label. This means the food has been taste-tested by cats and analyzed for digestibility.
- Read the label carefully for vague descriptors. *With lamb, chicken supper,* or *fish flavored* are often not the purest, healthiest choices for your feline.

BONUS BAG: Cats do not like their whiskers to touch the edge of the bowl! They will choose puddles or the toilet bowl if the water is too low in their dish. To avoid this, buy a dish with a bigger diameter or just keep the dish filled! If kitty still prefers the toilet, try substituting bottled or boiled water, or add a little club soda. Cats love carbonation!

- If the label says simply *chicken,* you can rest assured your cat is getting material exclusively from chickens. But that doesn't mean you're getting boneless chicken muscle; you're getting a defeathered, headless, footless, *eviscerated* chicken that's ground with the bones.
- If you buy meat by-products, like *chicken by-product,* the food will contain cleaned chicken *viscera* (think sausage casing), organ meats, and ground bones with adhering muscle that was not removed in the deboning process.
- Don't buy regular cat food for your kitten. Adult cat food is acidifying—which is good for older cats but can leach minerals from a kitten's growing bones. Cats over the age of seven may also benefit from less acidic diets. Check with your vet.
- Look for brands with taurine supplements to help your cat avoid heart problems and blindness later in life.

CAT LITTER

Don't buy scented cat litter! You might like it, but cats often don't. Their noses are too sensitive for those intense perfumes. Look for a cat litter that's nontracking (although there will always be some bits of litter to sweep up), dust free, and clumping for the easiest cleanup. The cheapest brand should do the job just fine. But don't buy clumping cat litter for a kitten. If they ingest it, they can choke. Wait until your cat is at least six months old to introduce clumping litter. Many vets also recommend recycled paper litter. It's gentle on cats' paws and dust and odor free. And remember, the number one reason a cat will refuse to use its litter box is that it smells bad. Can you blame them?

CHAMPAGNE

- Real champagne comes only from the Champagne region in France. Anything else is sparkling wine (known as *cava* in Spain). You'll pay more for the real thing, but because production rules are so strict, it's a safe bet you're getting a great vintage. A stamp from the Appellation d'Origine Controlée (AOC) certifies the bottle was made according to regulation.
- The word "nonvintage" on the label means the grapes come from several different vineyards over different seasons. By

AOC regulations, no producer can use more than 80 percent of their grapes for vintage champagne, which means there's lots left over to make high-quality nonvintage bottles.

- If you're inexperienced with champagne, we recommend starting with nonvintage rather than vintage bottles. You'll pay a lot more for vintage, and an unsophisticated palate may not appreciate its complexity and price tag.

- The word *cuvée* on the label indicates the winemaker has added a personal blend of several—sometimes dozens of—aging wines after the initial fermentation process.

- *Brut* is an indicator of dryness. It ranges from extra brut (bone dry) to extra dry (a little sweeter) to sec (medium sweet) to demi sec (medium sweet to sweet).

- Looking for a good sparkling wine? Look for ones that are made in the exacting *methode champenoise* standards. Our sommeliers say Spain and California make great ones.

SHOPPING BAGS VERDICT: To see if people could tell the difference between champagne and sparkling wine, we crashed a bunch of parties, including a film wrap party, a baby shower, and a wedding reception. Nine out of ten people preferred the champagne to the sparkling wine. And as champagne lovers, we have to agree—nothing tastes as good as the real thing!

CHEESE

- Goat cheese is sharp, sheep's milk cheese is very rich, and cheese made from cow's milk is blander by comparison—but varieties and flavors abound!

- Many cheese lovers say unpasteurized or raw-milk cheeses have the best flavors, but U.S. pasteurization laws require these cheeses to be aged for sixty days before they can be imported.

- Shop at stores with high turnover for maximum freshness.

- Buy cheese that's freshly cut from the block, rather than pre-cut, for the best flavor.

- If possible, take a whiff. The distinct scent of ammonia can be a sign the cheese is overripe. You can still eat it, but you may not find it that pleasant. (But keep in mind that some of the finest cheeses in the world smell strong.) If we see mold, we just cut it off and keep eating.

CHICKEN

- Make sure the package of chicken you choose hasn't been stacked above the top of the refrigerator case in the grocery store, which would mean it's not actually being refrigerated at all. Always choose one from near the bottom of the pile. Don't forget to check the expiration date.
- Avoid chicken with bruises or excessive blood spots. They can be signs of lower-quality meat.
- Flesh color is not necessarily an indicator of quality. Chicken farmers manipulate flesh color through feed and processing to make the product look more attractive to shoppers.
- Something labeled *organic* indicates the chicken has been raised on organic, pesticide-free feed and has not received any antibiotics. Beware of any other terms like *natural* or *no additives* or *no antibiotics*—they aren't regulated terms.

SHOPPING BAGS VERDICT: Our testers preferred the taste of organic chicken. Everyone found it juicier than regular chicken.

- Avoid packages that have a lot of liquid or even the faintest smell. Those are warning signs the chicken has seen better days.
- For the best price and the best flavor, buy chicken with the bone in. (It's juicier.)
- A *whole cut-up* chicken can contain parts from different birds.
- If possible, make chicken (and all other fresh meats, for that matter) the last thing you pick up in the grocery store—especially in the summer, when it's hot and meat goes bad quickly.
- Water-cooled chicken can absorb water, which adds to the weight, and some say dilutes the taste. But we didn't find a big difference in taste from water-cooled to air-cooled chicken.

CHOCOLATE

- For the best-quality chocolate, look for an ingredient label that shows a bar has 55 to 70 percent cocoa solids. (If you're not accustomed to the strong flavors of bittersweet chocolate, you might want to start with a bit less.)

- Bittersweet or dark chocolate contains less fat than milk chocolate.

- Some 92 percent of Americans prefer the taste of milk chocolate—something to keep in mind if you're gift giving.

FAST FACT: U.S. consumers eat 2.8 billion pounds of chocolate annually, representing nearly half the world's supply.

- Specialty chocolate has a shelf life of about two weeks, while mass-produced chocolate has more preservatives and a shelf life of about eight weeks. (You can tell it's stale when it has a white, chalky appearance.)

- Avoid buying chocolate that has white patches or looks dull in color. It could be past its prime. (Though we'd probably eat that stuff, too—if we had to, that is.)

- Fair-trade chocolate is another option to consider. This means that the farmers received a good price for their beans. (See the "Coffee" entry below for more information.)

COFFEE

- There are basically two types of beans. Arabica beans are handpicked and grown high in the mountains in a purer environment, where chemical fertilizers or pesticides are not usually needed. Robusta beans grow at lower altitudes, on plains where machine harvesting is easier and chemical fertilizers are used to help increase volume.

- Need a serious caffeine boost? Buy robusta beans, which pack about twice the caffeine as Arabica.

- If you prefer to buy ground coffee, buy from a specialized coffee shop to ensure you're getting the same type of bean rather than a blend. Otherwise, invest in a grinder and buy whole beans.

- Aroma is the quickest way to check for quality. If you don't already have a brand you like, shop at a store where you can smell the various types.

- *Estate brand* means the coffee has all come from the same area. This reduces the risk of lesser-quality beans being mixed in.
- Coffee comes in *light, medium,* or *dark* roast, with the latter having the fullest flavor.
- Inspect the beans. Their appearance will depend on how they're processed, which might not be indicated on the label. As a general rule, coffee beans from South America and east Africa are *wash processed* and will appear whole and uniform in shape. If they're *naturally processed*—like those hailing from Indonesia—they'll be less even, come in different sizes, and may even be broken. Both types of processing can make excellent coffee.
- Fair trade coffee is becoming more widely available. To be certified *fair trade* by TransFair USA, coffee farmers and workers have to receive a sufficient price for their beans under direct long-term contracts, use ecologically sustainable growing methods, and meet specific labor guidelines.

FAST FACT: Four hundred million cups of coffee are consumed daily in the United States. No wonder we import more than a third of the world's coffee!

- Beware of bogus marketing claims and misleading green terms like *fairly traded.* Unless you see the FAIR TRADE CERTIFIED label or the FAIR TRADE FEDERATION logo on a product, you can't guarantee you're buying the real thing.

DOG FOOD

- Most, but not all, commercial dog foods are formulated to the standards set by the American Association of Feed Control Officials (AAFCO). As with cat food, these guidelines offer the *minimum* requirements necessary for a dog's nutritional health, so look for statements on the package that indicate it "meets or exceeds the guidelines set forth by the AAFCO" to ensure the food is nutritionally complete.
- Read the label. Look for specific types of meat listed first, like chicken or beef. Then note the number of grain ingredients that follow. If there are several listed, there may be more grain than meat in the food.

- *Meat meal* is meat that has been cooked and dried and ground before processing into the dog food. Because meat that has not been cooked and dried can fall away, deteriorate, or evaporate during processing, meat meal means more meat for your dog.
- *Meat by-products* can refer to organ meat or other cuts that are not normally used by North American humans. Find out what the manufacturer uses for their by-product—some cuts are less digestible than others.
- Check for a guaranteed analysis of content on the side of the bag or can. This is an itemized explanation of the nutritional elements found within the product.
- Look for the words *feeding trial*. This means the food has been taste-tested by dogs and then analyzed for digestibility by looking at the dogs' blood and urine and amino acids (among other indicators).
- There is some evidence that dry foods do a better job of cleaning teeth than canned wet foods, but the use of dry food doesn't mean you can ignore your pooch's dental health.
- Some dog owners and veterinarians are proponents of the bones and raw food diet (BARF). They argue that live enzymes in raw foods help the digestion of nutrients and bacteria, and provide a healthier lifestyle for your dog—prolonging life, reducing arthritis and allergies, and eliminating toxins. But the BARF diet is expensive and controversial. Be sure to consult your veterinarian and shop for BARF diet items at a specialty store only.

ENERGY DRINKS

- Look for energy drinks that contain electrolytes, which are lost during exercise. We need electrolytes to maintain a healthy blood pressure level. Electrolytes speed the uptake of fluid from your stomach to your muscles, keeping all systems go. But for most of us, good old-fashioned water will do the trick just fine. You probably need to turn to an energy drink fortified with electrolytes only if you exercise for more than ninety minutes at a time or in the heat. (Most major brands do contain electrolytes, but some imitation energy drinks may just contain glucose, so you'll want to double-check.)

- Some drinks advertise being lower in carbohydrates than others. But keep in mind that this will also mean they're lower in calories and therefore provide less energy.
- Sport drinks that are to be consumed during exercise should max out at 6 percent carbohydrates, and no more than 120 milligrams of sodium per eight ounces. Energy drinks with more than 6 percent carbohydrates are considered recovery drinks and should be consumed *before* or *after* a workout but not during.
- Unless you're exercising for so long that you're skipping meals, your energy drink does not need to contain protein.
- Added vitamins aren't required. You don't burn vitamins any faster when you're exercising, and they may add to the price tag.

BONUS BAG: Save money by making your own energy drink. Add three tablespoons of sugar, an eighth of a teaspoon of salt, and a squeeze of lemon to your water bottle. (You may have to adjust the measurements for taste.)

- While energy drinks that require mixing with water may seem like a hassle, many serious athletes like them because they can adjust concentration levels as desired.
- Some "energy" drinks contain added caffeine, which actually promotes dehydration. Not a good choice for athletes. As always, read the label.

ENERGY BARS

Be sure to compare the protein, carbohydrates, fat, and fiber content (our nutritionists say at least two grams of fiber per bar is best) of various bars. And consider your lifestyle and exercise regimen. If you want to boost your energy level from time to time, go for a balanced bar (15 percent to 25 percent protein, 55 percent to 60 percent carbohydrates, and 20 percent to 30 percent fat). But if you want the bar to help you through a long workout (sixty minutes or longer), choose a high-carbohydrate bar. Trying to put on muscle mass or don't get enough protein in your diet? Buy a protein bar. And remember, most energy bars are rich in vitamins and minerals and require a lot of water to break down. Drink up!

GIN

- A label that says LONDON DRY is an indicator that the gin is very dry and has a strong juniper flavor. This style of gin is particularly good for mixing.
- If the label says PLYMOUTH, you can be assured of a more aromatic, sweeter gin, made with seven different botanicals.
- If you prefer a gin that's particularly light and fruity, try a Dutch brand. It's distilled from a malted grain mash similar to that used for whiskey.
- Paying more usually gets you a "smoother" gin, but that doesn't necessarily mean you'll prefer the taste. Also, remember that many of the higher-priced products have higher alcohol contents. (Which could be either a good thing or a bad thing!)
- On a low-carb diet? Gin may be a good choice if you're looking for an alcoholic refreshment. One ounce of 80 proof gin has 65 calories and no carbohydrates.

BONUS BAG: There are lots of possibilities when it comes to gin cocktails, but we adore the classics: the Gimlet (two ounces of gin, a quarter ounce of lime juice, and a scoop of crushed ice) and of course, the gin and tonic (tonic water added to two ounces of gin). Don't forget the lime wedge.

LUNCHEON MEAT

- Most luncheon meats contain high levels of salt—some contain more than 400 milligrams in one slice alone—and that's not good for anyone keeping tabs on their blood pressure. Plus, high amounts of sodium can cause bloating, and who needs that? A heart-healthy or low-sodium diet limits daily salt intake to 2,000 milligrams. Keep that range in mind as you compare labels.
- *Mechanically separated meats* means the meat was removed from the bones by machine. These meats can have a gritty quality due to small bone particles. Yuck!
- *By-products* or *variety meats* means the product may contain hearts, lips, tongue, and so forth. Double yuck!
- Sodium nitrate is a salt that's added to enhance a meat's color and flavor. During curing, *nitrate* can turn into *nitrite,*

which can then react with amines in the stomach to produce cancer-causing nitrosamines. However, nitrites are very effective anti-bacterial agents that can prevent botulism. For this reason, our food chemist says the benefits of nitrites outweigh the risks.

- Deli meats may seem healthier, but remember that they, too, were packaged at one point and probably contain nitrates and nitrites.
- For the healthiest choice, we recommend going with deli meats that are cooked fresh on the premises.

BONUS BAG: You can reduce the risk of nitrite conversion by eating more vitamin C with your lunch. Add a slice of tomato to your sandwich, or eat a piece of fruit afterward. (Some lunch meat manufacturers now add vitamin C to their meats for this reason.)

MAYONNAISE

- To be called mayonnaise, a product must contain 65 percent oil, plus eggs and vinegar or lemon juice.
- Less than 65 percent oil, and the product is labeled something like *mayonnaise-type dressing*—though by FDA definition, it's actually just salad dressing with added thickeners and emulsifiers. Miracle Whip and fat-reduced mayonnaise like Hellmann's (Best Foods) Light are salad dressings.
- Low-calorie and fat-reduced products often have added salt to maintain flavor. If you're watching your sodium intake, read the label.

- There can be a 500 percent price difference among brands. Though mayo is made up of a few basic ingredients, added secret seasonings mean the taste varies among products. Buy small containers until you find a product you like.
- Mayonnaise is actually healthier than butter or margarine. It contains less fat and calories and has no nasty trans fats. And Miracle Whip

SHOPPING BAGS VERDICT: We agree with our testers—you just can't beat Hellmann's (Best Foods) Mayonnaise!

(though not considered true mayonnaise) has 33 percent less fat than regular mayo.

MUSHROOMS

- Know the signs of freshness: Button mushrooms should be white, plump, and blemish-free, and the gills should be closed. Cremini or brown mushrooms should have smooth tops with edges that turn in slightly. Shiitakes should be firm and dry. Portobello mushrooms should have light brown, not black, gills. Oyster mushrooms should have smooth, not frayed, edges.

- The stems of chanterelle mushrooms often hold water. Give the stem a gentle squeeze so you're not paying for extra weight.

- When shopping, put mushrooms in a paper bag. Plastic makes them go slimy. Unless you're using them for dinner that night, repackage those prepacked mushrooms once you get them home.

BONUS BAG: Don't soak fresh mushrooms in water. They absorb water like little sponges and become limp and taste bland. A quick rinse will clean them easily.

- Use your nose to spot freshness. There should be no ammonia or musty odor.

- To save money, combine button or cremini mushrooms with more exotic types. They'll absorb some of the flavor during cooking.

- Can't afford truffles? Go with truffle oil.

- Consider dried mushrooms. While they need to be rehydrated thirty minutes ahead of cooking time, the flavor is more concentrated. And because they don't go bad, they're a good option for occasional cooks who like stocked pantries.

MUSTARD

- Look for mustard that comes in a bottle with a small neck. Mustard loses flavor when it comes in contact with air, so eat that opened jar fairly quickly.

- You can tell a lot about how mustard will taste by its color. Most American mustards are made from white mustard seeds and taste slightly sweet. Turmeric is added to give it that yellow color.

- French mustards are made with brown seeds and have a more pungent taste.
- English mustards are made with a combination of black, brown, and white mustard seeds. The resulting flavor is spicy and complex.
- Flavored mustards (like those with added spices or honey) often have more additives and preservatives than regular mustard.
- In France, only mustard that's made in Dijon can be called *Dijon mustard*. Others must be referred to as *Dijon-style mustard*. North American companies like French's use variations of the old Dijon recipes, but they don't have to follow the same labeling requirements.

> I'm addicted to English mustard—I have it with everything.
>
> **–NIGELLA LAWSON,**
> **BESTSELLING AUTHOR AND HOST OF BBC'S** *NIGELLA BITES*

OLIVE OIL

- Extra virgin olive oil is considered the best. It has a perfectly balanced taste, the highest concentration of antioxidants of all the olive oil types, and an acidity level of less than 1 percent. The *virgin* indicates the oil has not been through a refining process, which can alter natural flavors and aromas.
- Virgin olive oil is less expensive and has a slightly stronger smell and acidity than extra virgin oils. But it's still a high-quality oil.
- Regular olive oil (also known as *pure*) is a blend of virgin olive oil and lower-quality refined olive oil, and proportions and prices vary.
- Olive-pomace oil is refined oil that is extracted from the olive residue that remains after pressing. It's the lowest grade of oil available—and the cheapest—and our experts do not recommend it for cooking.
- Look for olive oil that comes in a tinted jar or dark container. As with beer, the dark glass will protect the product from light and keep it from going rancid.

- Look for a best-before date. Quality olive oil will last between twelve and eighteen months.
- Color is not an indicator of quality. Excellent oils can be light gold or dark green.
- Don't be fooled by the words *cold pressed* or *first pressed*. They're not reliably regulated label descriptions.

FAST FACT: Greece produces one-fifth of the world's olive oil, falling behind Spain and Italy. But they consume the most: The average Greek consumes twenty quarts of olive oil a year!

PASTA

- We think the best pastas are made from semolina flour, which is ground from durum wheat. Pasta made with this type of flour is light yellow or golden in color. The vast majority of European pastas are made exclusively from semolina flour.
- Pastas made from a combination of semolina and regular wheat flour tend to be softer and starchier. These kinds of pastas are more commonly produced out of North American factories.
- Surprisingly, all our testers preferred the taste of dried pasta to fresh *and* they preferred the brands that came from Italy. So even when not in Rome, we prefer Italian pasta. We all found the fresh stuff tasteless and slightly mushy.
- Our Italian testers and pasta aficionados were adamant that you should buy fresh pasta only when it's stuffed. Otherwise, stick to dried.
- Colored pastas get their pigment from added beet, spinach, or tomato flavors. But they lose these flavors when boiled, so buy them for presentation purposes only.
- Good-quality pasta should not stick together when cooked.

BONUS BAG: Ditch that spoon and eat your pasta real Italian style! Our Italian sources say the proper way to eat pasta is to twirl a few strands around your fork using only the dish for leverage.

- When cooking, here's a good rule of thumb: Match the pasta to the sauce. Delicate angel hair pasta works well with a light sauce or just tossed with some Parmigiano-Reggiano and a little extra virgin olive oil. A chunky meat or veggie sauce works well with chunky pasta like penne or rotini. (See "Olive Oil" on page 148 and "Tomato Sauce" on page 157 for more details.)

PEANUT BUTTER

- To be called peanut butter, the product must contain at least 90 percent peanuts.
- Yes, regular peanut butter is high in fat, but it's mainly the good unsaturated kind.
- Lower-fat products have about 25 to 30 percent less fat than regular peanut butter *but* they often have the same number of calories.
- Commercial peanut butters often contain added sugar and oil. This oil is usually hydrogenated oil, one of the bad fats. It's used as an emulsifier, to blend things together.
- For the healthiest peanut butter, look for a product with as few ingredients listed as possible. Your best bet is just straight peanuts and salt.

FAST FACT: The average American child will eat 1,500 peanut butter sandwiches by the time he or she graduates from high school.

- If you do buy natural peanut butter, keep in mind that it's often less smooth than commercial brands, and needs refrigeration.
- Planning to make peanut butter cookies? Our culinary experts tell us to buy commercially prepared peanut butter. Natural peanut butter seems to make the cookies too dry.
- We've rarely had so many dissenting opinions about a product. Anna likes commercial brands best. Kristina likes natural peanut butter. Our testers liked natural peanut butter and the chunky, smooth, and light varieties of the commercial brands. So you'll have to sample them all to find out which brand and style you prefer.

PIZZA-FROZEN

- An average five-ounce slice of frozen cheese pizza has about 13 grams of fat; the average pepperoni slice has 20. To reduce fat intake, choose pizzas with vegetarian toppings and minimal cheese. To cut calories and carbs, go with thin crust.
- Check ingredients for hydrogenated oil, the bad kind of fat. It's often found in rising-crust pizzas.
- Those watching their salt intake should take note: Our lab tests showed that brands often had way more salt than was reported on the box—20 to 30 percent more! That means two pieces of the average frozen pizza puts you over your recommended daily allowance.

BONUS BAG: We recommend blotting your pizza with a piece of paper towel to soak up the oil. Doing that can save you as much as 14 grams of fat per pizza. Every little bit helps!

- Package permitting, check the toppings, and make sure they're of a good size and not dried out.
- Some meat toppings may contain nitrites, which have been linked to cancer. (See "Luncheon Meat" on page 145 for more on this topic.)

POPCORN

- Compare manufacturers. Many of the big-name brands are owned by the same parent company. For example, ConAgra Foods, Inc., owns Act II, Jiffy Pop, and Orville Redenbacher. The more flavors and styles the company comes up with, the more shelf space it can occupy.
- Check the pricing. Microwave popcorn costs about three times more than plain kernels.
- Read the ingredients. Microwave and stovetop popcorn often contain hydrogenated oils—and therefore unhealthy trans fats.
- Note the serving size. Microwave popcorn's serving size is often much smaller than regular popcorn. You could be getting much more fat than you think.

- Check the instructions for preparation. We found that in some cases, nutritional information was based on air popping. So if you pop loose kernels using oil, remember to take those additional calories into account.

- In our kernel-count test, the stovetop style had the most "old maids." (That's popcorn lingo for unpopped kernels.) In second place was microwaved popcorn. Since you can't see into the package, it's hard to gauge when the popcorn is ready, so you're often left with more unpopped kernels and that means less popcorn for your money.

- Prepopped popcorn often contains added flavoring like cheese, which can increase fat and calorie counts.

- We buy regular plain kernels. They're inexpensive, and you can control the amount and type of oil you add to it.

- Our taste testers agree that brand-name plain kernels taste best. But generics rated a close second, so consider them if you're looking to save.

SALT

- We like kosher salt for cooking. The flakier granules dissolve very rapidly, so you can tell quickly if you haven't added enough.

- Most of our taste testers preferred sea salt to regular table salt on salads and veggies, finding it had more punch and overall flavor. We think it's worthwhile to pay more for sea salt that's used as a condiment.

- The iodine added to most North American table salt gives it a slightly bitter taste. That's why many chefs prefer cooking with kosher salt or sea salt. The iodine can also interfere with pickling, so when submersing those cukes, use special "pickling" salt.

- Anticaking agents are often added to salt to help it flow freely. Most of these are colorless, odorless, and harmless.
- With some salts, you are paying for labor costs. For example, France's Fleur de Sel and Sel Gris are hand-collected. They're tasty, though.

SCOTCH

- To be labeled as scotch, the spirit must come from Scotland and must be distilled and aged for a minimum of three years.
- *Single malt* means the scotch is from one distillery. It contains malted barley, some caramel, and no other grain. Single malts are considered smoother than blended scotches.
- *Blended* scotches can be a mix of up to fifty single malt and grain whiskies, and sometimes water and color are added, as well.
- The taste of single malt depends a lot on where it's from. In the southern lowlands, the scotch is lighter and softer. In the eastern

FAST FACT: Scotch in barrels loses 1 to 2 percent of its content each year to evaporation. This loss is referred to by distillers as *the angels' share.*

Speyside, it is the sweetest. Scotch from the highlands in the north is considered delicate and complex, with some peatiness. (Peat moss is used as fuel to dry the malt.) Scotch from the west (also known as Islay) is heavy, smoky, and peaty. Look for references to these places on the label.
- Older scotch is smoother and more expensive. Scotch does not age after it's been bottled. So a twenty-two-year-old scotch will be twenty-two forever. If only we, too, could figure out a way to seal our youth in a bottle!
- Good scotch should be aged a minimum of ten years. We recommend ones that list the age on the bottle.
- For a quality blended scotch, look for *deluxe blend.* That means there are better, older scotches added to the mix.

The age of a blended scotch is determined by the youngest scotch used.

- To figure out how much alcohol a particular bottle contains, divide the proof number in half. For example, a 100-proof scotch is 50 percent alcohol.
- Cask-strength scotches are less diluted than other scotches, are richer, and pricier, and usually have a higher alcohol content, too.
- Cask strength, age, area of origin, single malt, or blended are all things to trust on the label. But be aware of terms that are nothing more than marketing gimmicks; *cigar malt* doesn't mean anything.

SPICES AND HERBS

- Fresh isn't always better than dried. Spices like oregano, bay leaves, and peppers do very well dried. Leafy herbs like basil, cilantro, and parsley are better fresh.
- Dried herbs and spices are more concentrated. If the recipe calls for fresh, use less if you're substituting dried.
- Herbs begin to break down as soon as they're harvested. Look for bright green leaves with no brown spots. And follow your nose—herbs should smell fresh and fragrant.
- For maximum flavor, buy whole spices in seeds or herbs in leaves, and then crush or grind them as needed.
- Examine the contents of the spice container closely. Color should not be faded. Seeds should be whole, not broken. Make sure they don't smell musty.
- After two to four years in the cupboard, spices need replacing. They don't go bad, per se, but their flavors weaken significantly.
- Buy in small quantities until you find brands you like. This also ensures freshness.

SHOPPING BAGS VERDICT: We cooked up a storm using fresh and dried oregano in spaghetti sauce and fresh and dried cinnamon on toast. In both cases, the majority of testers preferred the dried spices. We were surprised, too!

STEAKS

- A tasty steak will have some fat or *marbling* in it. Fat contains enzymes that enhance flavor. Look for a smooth grain of fat running through the meat, as opposed to individual

chunks of fat. Bone-in steaks usually have more fat, and hence more flavor.

- Grading is voluntary, but it will still give you a good idea of the kind of meat you're getting. Something labeled *select* is usually the lowest grade of steak available in supermarkets and has some marbling. *Choice* is the most common grade. It has more marbling and costs more. *Prime* is considered top of the line and is most often sold by quality butchers.

- Check the color. The freshest meat will be anywhere from light to bright cherry. The exception is vacuum-packed meat—it's dark purple until exposed to air.

- Avoid steak that looks shiny in the package or where the fat is no longer white.

- As with other meats, avoid packages that contain too much liquid. It usually means the meat has been frozen and thawed.

- Most beef is aged. Dry-aging is an older, now rarer process usually done only with prime beef. Wet-aging is more common today.

- If you are worried about BSE or mad cow disease, steak may be one of the healthiest ways for you to eat beef. Mad cow disease takes three to four years to develop, and most steaks come from cattle that are only about two years old. Also, mad cow is usually found in organs, and steaks are cut from muscle.

TEA

- All real tea comes from the same plant—the *Camellia sinensis*. Differences in taste come from the plant variety and how it's processed.

- With green tea, the leaves are simply picked and dried so the tea tastes most like the tea leaf in its natural state. To make oolong tea, the leaves are partially dried and then left to ferment. Black tea is left to ferment longest and is considered the most processed.
- Teas are graded according to leaf quality—there's whole leaf and broken leaf. Whole leaf takes longer to brew. Some broken-leaf teas are broken intentionally, to release flavors. These pieces will be fairly large.
- Most tea bags contain tiny pieces of tea leaves known as *fannings* and tea-leaf dust. These particles infuse quicker than larger pieces, but our tea connoisseurs say they don't taste as good. (In fact, most experts consider supermarket brands the "wieners" of the tea world because everything goes in the bag.)
- A good black tea will list its variety on the label, such as Ceylon, Darjeeling, Assam.
- Most packaged teas are a blend of different varieties. This is true of both English Breakfast and Irish Breakfast.
- Orange pekoe is not a kind of tea—it's a grading system that describes the size and physical condition of leaves. Something labeled *Orange Pekoe* is actually just a blend of black teas, usually hailing from south Asia.
- Herbal teas—also known as tisanes—are not real tea. They do not contain tea leaves, but are made with other plants, like chamomile and mint.
- All real tea contains caffeine. If you're watching your caffeine intake, buy green tea. It has the least caffeine, while black tea has the most.
- Bags are not cheaper! Loose tea is often less expensive on a cup-by-cup basis.

BONUS BAG: Tea bags are more likely to pick up flavors from surrounding foods in your cupboard than are loose-leaf teas. They also tend to go stale more quickly because of their much smaller tea-leaf particles. So toss the cardboard box, and store bags in a tightly sealed metal or opaque glass container to keep the tea at its tastiest.

TOMATO SAUCE

- Look for sauces with fresh, simple ingredients. The basics are tomatoes, oil, and spices. Tomatoes should come *first* on the ingredients list.
- Look for fresh herbs and spices versus powdered ones.
- A good sauce doesn't need fillers (like cornstarch).
- Tomatoes are very acidic, and therefore sauces shouldn't need preservatives to stay fresh.
- Many sauces have sweetener or corn syrup added. Make sure the sweetener is not too high on the ingredients list.
- Don't buy sauce with the cheese already in it—it's perishable. Add freshly grated cheese later.
- Our taste testers, a group of Italian mothers with strong opinions on tomato sauce, preferred a basic jarred sauce like Prego to gourmet sauces that were ten times the price.

> There is one little misconception that I want to make clear, and that is that for the best tomato sauce, you need to have fresh tomatoes. Not so. If in season and the tomatoes are ripe, fresh tomatoes are the best, but in the wintertime, when you don't have the ripe fresh tomatoes, canned tomatoes are excellent for a good sauce.
>
> **–LIDIA BASTIANICH,** HOST OF *LIDIA'S ITALIAN-AMERICAN KITCHEN*

TUNA

- According to FDA regulation, only albacore tuna can be labeled *white tuna,* though it can appear beige or light pink in color. It's usually packed in solid form and has a mild taste. Albacore is more expensive than other kinds of tuna, partly because it's labor-intensive to catch.
- You may see the term *fancy* on some cans of white tuna. This is just a, well, fancy term for solid white.
- *Light* tuna may have different types of tuna packed together, like skipjack, tongol, and yellowfin. It's usually cheaper, moister, less firm, and more "fishy" tasting than albacore.

- Chunk or flake tuna is the cheapest kind and accounts for nearly 70 percent of all tuna sales. Like "light" tuna, it may contain different types of tuna packed together. This style of canned tuna is the moistest of the bunch and can make for a soggy sandwich.

- If the can says it's packed in vegetable oil, that usually means soybean oil. Solid tuna absorbs less oil than flaked or chunk.

- *Dolphin free* sounds important, but it doesn't mean much. First, albacore tuna is not caught with nets, so dolphins aren't even jeopardized. Second, other types of tuna that are caught with nets do not always have this claim verified by independent agencies.

- We agree with our testers (fishermen) who preferred the taste of solid white tuna to other types. Anna swears by name brands, while Kristina can't tell the difference—but she does tend to defer to Anna in all matters relating to cooking.

TURKEYS

- A *free-run* turkey means the bird has been left to roam freely in the barn. *Free-range* means the turkey has been allowed to run around outside.

- Organic turkeys are raised on 100 percent organic feed exclusively and do not receive any antibiotics. These birds often cost twice as much as regular turkey.

- Toms (male birds) are usually bigger, longer, and heavier than hens. However, they have less fat and are therefore less juicy.

- *Grade A* doesn't refer to the quality of meat. A grade A bird is one that is physically perfect. You can save over 50 percent by buying a *utility bird*. This means it is physically imperfect—the skin is torn or a wing is missing.

- To find out if the bird is fresh, press the flesh with your finger. If it springs back quickly, it's a fresh turkey. We also recommend buying birds that are packaged the day you're shopping. Check the date on the label.
- Fresh birds are generally more expensive than frozen because you're paying for the convenience of not having to thaw it out.
- If you're buying a self-basting turkey and tend to be a health-conscious consumer, check the ingredients for unhealthy oils, such as palm oil.
- When deciding on size, the rule of thumb is one pound per person. But increase that ratio slightly if you want leftovers—and who doesn't?

SHOPPING BAGS VERDICT: To see if we could taste the differences among all these turkeys, we cooked up four twelve-pound birds for the harshest of food critics, our relatives. On the menu: a fresh bird, a frozen bird, a free-run turkey, and an organic turkey (fed only organic feed). The fresh, regular turkey was the unanimous favorite. Which just goes to show that you don't have to spend a bundle to have a great holiday feast. (Just remember to baste!)

WINE

- The *vintage* refers to the year the grapes were picked, not the year the wine was bottled.
- Don't buy into words like *reserve* and *barrel select.* These are just fancy-sounding marketing terms, and there's no guarantee the winery saved its best grapes for those bottles. The exceptions are wines from Italy and Spain, where reserve means the wine has received extra aging.
- *Estate bottled* means the grapes came from the winery's own vineyard, rather than independent growers or other vineyards. Whether *estate bottled* implies a superior-tasting, higher-quality wine is the subject of much debate.
- A *late harvest* means the grapes were picked later in the year, and they probably have a richer, more complex taste.

- Just because it has a screw cap doesn't mean it's bad. More and more wine producers, especially out of Europe, are turning to screw caps and plastic corks because of a worldwide shortage in cork supply. Really, the use of cork is just about tradition. It is not critical in the bottling and aging of wine.

- If you're looking to save money, consider a boxed wine from Down Under. They've been doing it since the 1960s, and they still do it best. We tried a chardonnay that wasn't half bad!

- Some whites are aged in oak barrels. This gives them a rich "toasty" and "buttery" flavor. (That's wine-speak.) Old-world wines are rarely oaked, so look for those if you don't like the taste of oak.

- Older isn't always better. Our wine experts say some wines are made for drinking in the first year, when they are fresh and crisp. (This is especially true of many whites.) But oaked wines are best when they spend some time in the bottle.

- White grapes 101: Chardonnay is a best-selling, versatile grape that can taste anywhere from rich and buttery to oakey and dry. Pinot grigio is very dry and acidic. Pinot gris is the same grape, but it can taste quite different depending on where it's grown. It has flavors of apple, apricot, peach, and honey. Sauvignon blanc is reminiscent of tangy citrus and green fruit. If you have a sweeter tooth, opt for Riesling or gewürztraminer.

- Red grapes 101: Cabernet sauvignon and Shiraz (aka Syrah) tend to be more full-bodied, earthy reds. Merlot—chardonnay's red cousin—is a popular, versatile grape that produces rich, sometimes chocolaty, medium-bodied wines. It is often blended with cabernet sauvignon. Pinot noir is lighter and more fragrant, often on the dry side, but with a soft berry fruit taste. Gamays (a famous export from France's Beaujolais region) are also fruity and on the sweet side.

CORKSCREWS

There are several different types of corkscrews, but our first choice is the waiter's style: it's easy and quick to use, inexpensive, and takes up less drawer space. This style also outperforms others when opening bottles with synthetic corks. Look for one that's two-tiered for extra leverage. Also, a corkscrew made of metal (especially stainless steel or zinc) will usually outlast one with plastic or resin parts. Whatever style you choose, make sure the worm (the spiral that pierces the cork) is sharp and thin, with smooth edges.

6. Playtime: Recreational Gear

Ever wonder if a composite hockey stick would improve your game? Looking for a tent that doesn't require a Ph.D. to put up? Or simply trying to find a pair of running shoes that won't leave you on the sidelines? We all love to get out and play, whether it's at the playground, the campground, or a local yoga studio. In this busy day and age, maximizing your free time is key and is made all the more enjoyable with the right gear, sporting goods, and gadgets for your lifestyle. The catch is, of course, that choosing the right gear *takes* time. We're going to make shopping for sporting goods a whole lot easier so that you can get out of the mall . . . and onto the mountain!

> Park at the back of the lot, and get a little extra exercise walking into the mall.

Like the cosmetics industry, the sporting goods business is rife with large companies that own smaller labels and product lines. For example, Nike owns Converse; Rawlings purchased Worth; and Callaway, the famous golf-club manufacturer, has taken over a part of the competition—namely Spalding Top Flite and Hogan. More and more retailers are also coming out with their own private labels.

All of this translates to good news for shoppers. There are more choices and more price points. When shopping for sporting goods, especially fitness equipment, keep this in mind: The markup is about 100 percent. You pay double what it cost the retailer to purchase the product from the manufacturer. So there's lots of room for retailers to negotiate on price.

When planning a vacation to somewhere exotic, find a travel agency that specializes in that country. It will have the inside scoop on the best airfares and what to do when you get there.

We find that when it comes to recreational gear, you usually *do* get what you pay for. There's no question the lighter, more expensive, titanium tennis racket will improve your game from the days when you played with a wooden racket. But it's not as simple as spending more. You've really got to know your body and your strengths and weaknesses in a given sport before buying any piece of equipment. Do you land on the inside of your foot (i.e. pronate) when you jog? You'll need a shoe with denser foam along the instep of the midsole. Are you a woman? Then you probably need more flexible golf clubs and skis.

A big part of finding the best product is testing it out. And that's the great thing about sporting-goods stores. Sales staff actually *expect* you to demo their wares. You can conduct your very own Shopping Bags test! (Recall Commandment #7—Kick the Tires.)

Outdoor-gear swaps are a great way to save money on camping gear and sporting goods *and* recycle your own. Search the Web for a swap near you. And if you use an online swap, you don't have to wait for the official swap to take place—you can shop, recycle, and save all year round.

It's even more important to check the merchandise when buying used. We believe going secondhand is a great idea, especially for growing kids or adults who are commitment-phobic when it comes to sports. Renting is always a good option when gauging interest, too. Before you buy, make sure the older model hasn't been recalled by the Consumer Product Safety Commission (www.cpsc .gov); you want good value *and* a safe and reliable product.

Until you are well versed in the sport and its equipment, we recommend going to the experts. That usually means specialty stores.

And if they sell stuff for only that one sport, that's even better. The guys at the snowboarding shop—the ones who live and breathe the sport—best understand the anatomy of the boards, the bindings, and the materials from which they're made.

One exception to this rule is buying sports clothing. Unless you are looking for gear to keep you warm on your next expedition to Everest, you can find good deals and quality products at department stores, outlet stores, and the like.

Whether you're a hard-core athlete, a weekend warrior, or a certifiable couch potato looking for a pair of comfy yoga pants to lounge around in, we're geared up to help you navigate all the aisles of the sporting-goods store.

HERE'S WHAT'S IN OUR SHOPPING BAG

BACKPACKS

- If you're planning on using a backpack for anything more than carrying books to school or for daily shopping errands, you'll need more than a simple daypack (which holds only 900 to 2,200 cubic inches).
- Fit is crucial. The right fit depends on the size of the pack and the suspension system, not on its capacity.
- To find your pack size, measure the distance from your most prominent neck vertebra to the low point between hip bones. If your torso is less than eighteen inches, you will probably require a small suspension system. Eighteen to twenty inches, and you'll need a medium suspension system, and twenty-one inches or more requires large.
- Get a pack with a waist belt for extra support. You won't win any fashion awards, but it takes the weight off your shoulders and is better for your back. Look for hip padding that wraps completely around the hip bones.
- Look for shoulder straps that are padded and contoured to fit the body, and make sure they are far enough apart that they don't squeeze your neck.
- Keep in mind that backpacks fit men and women differently, with women generally finding it more comfortable to carry weight lower down and closer to the hips. Many packs that

work for men don't adjust for a shapely woman's body. Be sure to try it on in the store! Most major brands make packs designed for women specifically, but you'll still want to examine whether the straps contour around your hips and chest comfortably. (Some men actually find women's packs more comfortable, so size and fit depend entirely on the wearer!)

- Front-loading packs have a large horseshoe-shaped zipper across the front. It allows you to peel back the whole front panel for easy access to all your belongings. Handy. But such a large zipper means a higher potential for water leakage.

- Top-loading packs are inherently stronger than front loaders, but finding a particular item can be more difficult.

- Take a close look at the stitching. Seams should be joined with closely spaced stitching, and stress points should be reinforced. Watch out for packs with too many panels. The more seams, the more places there are to wear out.

- A mesh panel will allow for airflow between you and your pack and prevent your back from getting too sweaty.

BONUS BAG: A word of caution—our experts inform us there's really no such thing as a waterproof backpack. While some high-end specialty packs for water sports like canoeing and kayaking do a better job at keeping water out, most packs will eventually leak. If you expect to hike in a wet climate, we highly recommend a pack cover.

THERMOSES

Stainless-steel thermoses are more expensive than plastic or glass ones, but in our tests, they were more durable and retained heat the best. To keep that hot chocolate toasty warm, look for a stopper with deep grooves, as shallow stoppers let more heat escape. And here's our hottest thermos tip: Don't buy one at a chain coffee shop (we won't name names, but you know who we're talking about), a car dealer, or anywhere else that puts their brand name on it. Most of these are exactly the same as ones for sale at a department store, minus the trendy name and the steeper price tag.

BASEBALL GLOVES

- Aside from specialized gloves for particular positions, the main difference from one glove to the next relates to quality and softness of the leather.

- If you're buying for a pitcher, outfielder, or third baseman, choose a glove with closed webbing. It provides more support and, in the case of the pitcher, it hides the ball so the batter can't see what kind of pitch might be coming.

- Gloves made with treated leathers don't require a breaking-in period, but they also break down faster and therefore don't last as long.

- Buy in the off season, and save up to 30 percent.

- Don't get sucked into paying a premium for a label you recognize. All brands make good-quality gloves.

- Don't buy gloves for children to grow into. If it's too loose, they won't be able to catch the ball and chances are they'll wind up disliking the sport. (This may explain why Kristina still can't play baseball to save her life.)

> I think once kids start getting a little older, around I'd say twelve or thirteen years old, and they're playing more competitive baseball, that's when they start needing specialized infielders' and outfielders' gloves.
>
> **–VERNON WELLS,**
> **STAR CENTER FIELDER**
> **FOR THE TORONTO**
> **BLUE JAYS**

BIKE LOCKS

- If buying a U-shaped lock (the most popular style), make sure the locking mechanism is in the center as opposed to the end. Center locks are harder to get to.

- Cable locks bend and are easier to use than U-shaped locks. Make sure the cable is at least three feet long and woven, making it harder to cut through.

- With a chain lock, make sure it's at least three-eighths of an inch thick and that the links are welded together. Also, it's harder for thieves to get their tools through square links than though round links.

- Some locks can get very heavy. Make sure you're comfortable carrying around this added weight.

- Whatever style you choose, bigger and thicker is better because it's harder to cut through. And make sure the lock is made of hardened steel.

- Keep in mind that no lock is absolutely safe. Spend about 10 to 15 percent of the value of your bike on the lock.
- For any thief, time is of the essence. Using two locks will help slow him down.
- Read the fine print on your guarantee, as sometimes the lock manufacturer will actually pay only a portion of the cost of a replacement bike.

BONUS BAG: Don't mount your U-lock onto your bike frame. Most mounts won't hold the lock securely in place, and they'll scratch your frame. Keep your lock in a backpack.

BIKES–MOUNTAIN

- Bikes go on sale in the late summer or early fall (notably the end of biking season in most states).
- If you're going to hit some serious trails, get a bike with dual suspension. This means the bike has shock absorbers in the front and back. Recreational or cross-country riders may need only front suspension or even a fully rigid bike.
- Generally speaking, the lighter the bike, the more expensive it is. Steel frames are heavy but durable. Look for CroMo or chromoly steel—it's high-quality steel.
- Aluminum frames are lighter and have come down in price significantly in recent years. When looking at aluminum frames, remember—the lower the alloy number, the lighter the frame.
- Titanium and carbon-fiber bikes are the lightest and most durable, but also the most expensive.
- Make sure the bike fits. Stand with the bar between your legs. You need three to four inches of clearance. You should feel comfortable, not too stretched out or cramped.
- We recommend shopping at a specialty bike shop. They'll be able to fit you properly, plus you'll have somewhere to go if you need repairs. Specialty shops also include service warranties that typically cover tune-ups and adjustments for the first year you own your bike. (You'll need it. Our experts say

you'll probably need to take your bike in for a tune-up three to four times during the breaking-in period.)

BIKE HELMETS

Finding the right bike helmet is all about fit. It should sit snugly, so that it moves with your head, but not so tight as to give you a headache. Wear it straight across your brow bone to protect your forehead in case of a forward spill. And ensure that the straps are fairly snug under your chin so that if you fall back, the helmet doesn't fall off. All bike helmets sold in the United States must meet federal safety standards set by the Consumer Product Safety Commission. Check the Web site for any product recalls or safety updates: www.cpsc.gov.

EXERCISE BIKES

- There are two basic choices when it comes to style. An upright bike is designed to ride like a road bike, whereas a recumbent bike has a backrest that allows you to sit back like in a chair. Upright bikes are usually slightly cheaper.
- An upright bike works the quadricep muscle at the front of the thigh, and the hamstrings in the back. But to really work those hamstrings, you'll need to use toe clips.
- The recumbent bike works more like a leg press, working the glute muscles in your butt, hamstrings, and quads. So overall, the recumbent style bike works a larger muscle mass.
- Consider where you'll put the bike. Recumbent bikes are usually bigger and heavier. This is something to keep in mind if you'll be moving the bike around.
- When trying various bikes in the store, pay attention to the following characteristics: noise, smoothness (at various levels), stability, size (does it adjust to fit you?), and comfort (most important, the seat).
- Many inexpensive bikes are made with a *flywheel*—a heavy wheel with a weight strap tightened around it that provides resistance. In our tests, many people found this style of bike noisy and uncomfortable to ride. And when it's set at the higher resistance levels, it can feel like you're riding with the brakes on.

- Bikes made with a *magnetic frictionless* resistance system are relatively quiet and allow for the greatest variety of resistance levels. But they're also more expensive than flywheel models.
- If the bike has a monitor, make sure it's easy to read and that the settings can be easily adjusted while you're riding.
- If you have children around, look for a shrouded wheel so little fingers don't get pinched.
- The heavier the wheel, the more stable the bike. But make sure a bike with a heavy wheel also has casters to help with moving it around.

EXERCISE CLOTHING

- Look for an extra hanging label attached to a garment to tell you exactly what you're getting. The label sewn onto the collar usually doesn't reveal much.
- For optimum performance, look for fabric that is both hydrophobic (water repellent) and that wicks sweat away from the body and allows it to evaporate.
- If you can't deal with high-maintenance laundry, make sure you read the washing instructions before you buy. Some garments allow you to throw them in the dryer, while others suggest they be hung to dry.
- Make sure you get the right fit. If something is too big, it won't wick away sweat properly.
- Look for a fabric that will work in a variety of weather conditions. You can usually tell by the number of insulation layers or by the hangtags, which often give an optimum temperature range.

EXERCISE GIZMOS

- We don't recommend buying from infomercials. Whether it's an ab roller or butt cruncher, it's impossible to gauge quality if you can't actually try out the device. And even if you can return it, you'll still have to pay shipping costs.

- Manufacturer promises of *fitness made easy* or *abs of steel* may be tempting, but motivation doesn't come in a box. Even if the item is effective, you're the one who has to do the actual work. So consider your level of commitment before you open your wallet.

- We recommend visiting your local gym and experimenting with similar equipment to see if you feel comfortable with it. Can you see yourself using it months or years down the road?

- Find out how much assembly is required, as some exercise gizmos come with lots of parts. Putting them together can be a workout in itself!

SHOPPING BAGS VERDICT: We've tested quite a few of these products, and we've come up with some general findings: Abdominal machines don't work any better than doing plain old sit-ups. Leg and butt machines don't work any better than leg lifts or squats. Cardio gizmos can be good at raising heart rate and inducing a sweat. But it's often hard to change settings because many machines use hydraulic pistons, and you have to get off the machine to change resistance.

- If you're just starting out, don't choose an exercise gizmo that promises improvement in targeted areas. The key is just to start moving. Machines that focus on individual areas, like your stomach or butt, don't do as much for overall health.

- Many exercise gizmos come with specific promises to tone and reduce weight. But know that a strict diet plan is also often part of the deal. Don't expect miracles!

GOLF CLUBS

- If you're just taking up the sport, learn the basics of which clubs you'll need in your new bag. Woods are the longest clubs with the large bulbous heads, and they're designed to send the ball a far distance. Irons have the greatest variety;

low-numbered ones are for longer distances, while higher-numbered irons are used to arc the ball shorter distances. A putter is used on the green to tap the ball a few feet into the hole. (At least, that's the theory!)

- Golf pros we talked to say getting professionally fitted for your clubs is far more important than spending a lot on clubs made with specialty materials, like titanium.
- If you're on a budget, go for a steel shaft. In fact, many pros prefer a steel shaft because it's heavier. But the more expensive graphite is good for seniors and new golfers because it's lighter, more flexible, and more responsive.
- Pay attention to grip size. If it's too small, you'll have a tendency to turn your hands over through impact. If it's too big, you might have trouble rotating your hand through the ball, which results in a slice.
- Make sure you get the right flex level for your ability—it'll help you keep control of the ball. Women tend to have a slower swing speed and therefore need a more flexible shaft.
- Be sure to buy clubs that are the right length for your body. Sawing off the ends of your dad's old set just won't do it. If you're a woman five feet eight inches or taller, consider a men's-length shaft in a lighter flex.
- Don't buy until you've tried several different sets. Rent clubs the first few times out, or borrow from a friend who is of similar weight, height, and strength as you. Also, inquire about demoing clubs from a specialty shop. If you wind up buying, the shop should take the demo price off the sticker price.

> I've never been a fan of belly or long putters, because I don't think anything should be anchored to the body. I think the art of putting is trying to figure out how to coordinate your arms, wrists, and shoulders and hands to swing the blade, and I think that's part of the game of golf.
>
> **–TIGER WOODS**

HIKING BOOTS

- If you prefer to pack light or if you are just looking for a shoe for walking, trail running, or light hiking, buy a lightweight hiker. They're like runners with a heavier sole and will support you and your daypack for a few hours. Most are not waterproof. Look for an ankle or low-top shoe with flexible, well-cushioned soles.

- If you're going on full-day hikes over variable terrain, look for a waterproof backpacking boot. They can support a pack up to roughly thirty pounds. In backpacking boots, look for a rigid heel cup and solid toe box as well as a quarter-inch steel shaft for added support. All that said, this boot must still be supple enough to stay comfortable for long walks along the trail.

- If you're going hiking for several days at a time with a heavy pack, buy heavyweight hikers. Look for stiff above-the-ankle support, leather, and few seams.

- If you plan to be scaling mountains (which we often do to get to a good sale), you'll need some mountaineering boots. They're very stiff and highly specialized. These boots are leather, waterproof, and can support one hundred pounds (of shopping bags perhaps!). Look for full-grain leather and a sole that is curved for comfort, also known as a *rockered* sole. Remember that these boots are heavy-duty and will need an extended breaking-in period. That means wearing them around the house and on shorter hikes before the big excursion.

- Don't shop online or at discount malls, where often the staff people aren't very knowledgeable. Getting the right fit is critical here, so we recommend shopping at a specialty store. A salesperson should take several different measurements of your feet to ensure the right fit.

- Be sure to shop with the socks you'll wear when you go hiking. Mountaineering experts recommend wool or synthetic fabrics, which do a better job of preventing blisters. Don't wear 100 percent cotton! When your cotton socks get wet from sweaty feet, they take forever to dry.

- If you have narrow feet, expect your shopping trip to take a little longer, as most boots are designed for medium-width feet.
- Try to shop at the end of the day, when your feet are their most swollen, just as they will be after a few hours of hiking. It will help you get a good fit.
- Look for as few seams as possible. A one-piece upper (everything above the sole) is the most waterproof.
- Consider the pattern on the soles of the boot (also known as the *lugs*). The lugs are designed to provide traction. If you're going on hikes with more hazardous terrain, you'll need deeper lugs.

HOCKEY STICKS

- Wooden sticks are a good bet if you're a beginner or intermediate player, as they cost less than composite sticks.
- Buy a wood stick with a solid core. Those that are just laminated fiberboard can break with the first serious slap shot.
- More advanced players prefer composite sticks, which are made from graphite compounds. They are much lighter and stronger and therefore more consistent than wooden sticks, but they are also much more expensive.
- A middle-of-the-road option is a composite shaft with a changeable wooden blade.
- Borrow as many different types of sticks as possible, and try them out on the ice before you buy.
- Getting the right length is very important. When you're standing in bare feet, the stick should come to just under your nose.
- Flexibility is important because it relates to the stiffness of the shaft. It's this stiffness that transfers the power from your body to the puck. A stick with a rating of 50 means it takes fifty pounds to make the shaft bend one inch. Professional hockey players use sticks with a

> Young kids, they always want a big curve in their hockey stick because the first thing they want to do is lift the puck. They think that's cool, but it's also harder to control the puck. So for younger kids just starting out, I think a mild curve would be perfect for them.
>
> **–SHELLEY LOONEY,** HOCKEY PLAYER, 2002 U.S. OLYMPIC TEAM, WOMEN'S HOCKEY

flex rate of around 110. A flex rate of 75 or 80 is fine for most women.

- Blades come in different curves, shapes, and sizes (known as the *pattern*). The curve is the most important factor here. A greater curve allows you to lift the puck and put spin on it, but it can make it more difficult to shoot or pass backhand. Rookie players should choose a less curved blade.

- Check the *lie* of various sticks. (That's the angle of the shaft to the blade.) The higher the number, the steeper the lie. So if you skate bent over or are on the short side, you'd probably prefer a lower lie.

- Make sure the grip is the right size for your hands. Some manufacturers are recognizing women's interest in the sport (finally!) and making smaller grips.

HOT TUBS

- Portable tubs—as opposed to the in-ground variety—are the easiest to install. They are also energy efficient, less expensive, and, as the name implies, you can take them with you when you move.

- Look for an acrylic tub with a granite surface. Acrylic is durable and easy to maintain, and the granite finish hides scratches and water spots better than a marble finish.

- Make sure your hot tub has between seven and ten layers of fiberglass. Any less and the shell could crack or break.

- Lights are a great feature to have if you entertain at night and want to set the mood. We think they're worth the extra cost.

- Buy a tub with an ozone system or one that's *ozone-ready* so you have the option of installing the system later. Ozone systems purify water and reduce the amount of chemicals needed to keep the tub water clean. They save you money on chlorine and minimize that distinct chemical smell that goes along with hot tubs.

- Ensure your hot tub comes with a rigid cover. They're safer than the flexible ones and do a better job of holding in heat. Look for covers that have been reinforced with aluminum channel.

- Deep tubs keep you toasty right up to your neck but remember, they will cost you more over the long term. One way to cut the monthly heating bill is to buy a tub with full foam insulation. It'll cost you more up front, but ultimately save you money.

- Take your swimsuit to the store, and actually test out the hot tubs. Any specialty store will fill up a tub for you. It's a tough job testing hot tubs!

- More jets aren't necessarily better. Instead go for widely spaced, adjustable high-performance jets. Also look at the placement or pattern of the jets. Some tubs have jets arranged differently at each seat so you get a different massage at each station. This is a good feature to have if you're using the tub for hydrotherapy purposes.

- Many stores carry only one brand, so be sure to shop around.

HEALTH ALERT:
Don't use a hot tub if you're pregnant. The hot water can raise your body temperature too high, and that's not good for baby.

ICE SKATES

- Make sure you can bend your ankles when you try on the skates. As a novice skater, you need the leather boot to be stiff enough to provide support, but not too unforgiving. Really high-end skates are very stiff and meant for advanced skaters, so save your money until you can do toe jumps and sit spins.

- If buying skates for a child, don't get a size too big for "growing into." Little feet won't sit properly on the blade, making skating more difficult. And that means there's a good chance those figure skates will collect dust.

- Don't buy skates with Velcro fasteners. Lace-ups do a better job of tightening and staying put.

- Most skates come with boot and blade attached. Don't buy them separately until you're a serious skater.

- North American— and European-brand ice skates have a high-quality reputation.

- Once you've chosen your skates, have the store *heat-mold* them for you. If you shop at a specialty store, they'll do this for free. This heat process molds the boot to your exact foot shape, shortening the painful breaking-in period.

- Beginner skaters should choose a skate with a small pick. Larger picks are meant for jumping and will only trip you up if you're just getting started. (Anna swears this is why she never made it to the Olympics—her pick was too big!)

- Look for boots that are screwed to the blade, not riveted. That way the blade can be adjusted or replaced if it wears out.
- Buying used skates can be a great way to save money. Examine the toe crease. The bigger it is, the more broken down the skate is. Also examine the wear on the blade by comparing it to a brand-new skate.

INLINE SKATES

- Look for a soft boot over a hard one for the best fit.
- Laces might not provide enough support for a beginner. You may want to try out a few pairs with buckles instead. Look for at least three adjustment options to ensure the best fit. (Note: buckle-fastened skates are not typically carried at specialty inline skate stores.)
- The larger the wheels, the faster the roll. The smaller the wheels, the more stable and easier the skates are to maneuver.
- Check out the wheel hardness. Harder wheels last longer and go faster on rough surfaces, whereas softer wheels provide better shock absorption and do a better job of gripping surfaces.
- Ball bearings (found on the inside of the wheels) will determine how smoothly the wheels turn. Be sure to buy wheels with an ABEC rating (Annular Bearing Engineer Council). Inferior wheels won't have an ABEC rating.

JACKETS—OUTDOOR RECREATIONAL

- Make sure the jacket is waterproof as opposed to water-resistant, or you'll get wet in anything heavier than a light shower. Also check that the jacket material is breathable—that way you won't get clammy.

- Covered or treated zippers, as well as zipper "garages," will help keep out moisture.
- Try on the hood to make sure it fits properly, as they can often be too big for women's heads. You don't want your hood to fly off when moving quickly (think downhill skiing), and make sure the hood doesn't limit peripheral vision.
- Underarm vents are a great idea if you'll be wearing the jacket during more active outdoor sports. They help cool you down when you're working hard.
- Inside pockets are a good feature if you're carrying anything that needs extra protection (like a cell phone or sunglasses).
- Check the seams. Double stitching will help prevent tearing, while taped seams seal out water.

KAYAKS

- A recreational kayak (also known as an ocean or sea kayak) is an all-around kayak good for weekend outings and calm waters. Touring or expedition kayaks are bigger, with room for storage. Whitewater kayaks are shorter, designed for maneuverability in rapids.
- Kayaks made of polyurethane plastic are relatively inexpensive and durable, but they're heavy. We like fiberglass kayaks because they're lighter and faster, but they're also more expensive. Kevlar (a polymer) boats are pricey but strong and light, making them easier to carry and maneuver.
- Folding kayaks are a good option for those with little storage space, but they are the most expensive type. (Don't worry, they don't leak.)
- Check the length of the boat. A longer boat will go faster and "track better," meaning it glides more smoothly than a shorter boat.
- The wider the kayak, the more stable it is. While this may sound appealing to beginners, if a kayak is super stable, it actually takes more

SHOPPING BAGS VERDICT: To test the stability of kayaks, we took a couple to an indoor wave pool. Although our wider plastic kayak was less tippy than the longer, narrower Kevlar one, we learned that you can overturn pretty much any kayak with just a little bit of effort. And you know what? It's actually kind of fun! (As long as you're not in rushing rapids!)

work to move it. Once we got over our fears, we actually preferred a long, narrow boat.

- A double kayak is less expensive than two singles, and it's a
good choice if you want to kayak with someone who's at a
different skill level than yours. But doubles are often referred
to as *divorce boats*. We started bickering, and we're not even
married!

LUGGAGE

- If the luggage has wheels, make sure they're inset and not
just fastened to the frame. Wheels attached to the outside
tend to break off more easily. And check out the extendable
handle. Does it come up to a height that will be comfortable
for you? We like handles that swivel—they take the weight
and stress off your wrist as you roll your way through the ter-
minal.
- Look for a suitcase made with ballistic nylon for ultimate
durability and strength. Vinyl should be avoided.
- Hard-sided bags made of ABS plastic crack easily (especially if you subject them to a bumper car crash test as we
did!). Polypropylene is a better choice.
- Don't use locks. Anything that dangles or hangs off your
suitcase can get caught in luggage handling systems and
fall off. They don't provide any worthwhile security either.
(Plus, the airport will break open the lock if the bag has to be
screened for security purposes.)
- Look for a large zipper with strong teeth. Thin zippers made
of nylon won't stand up well to an overloaded suitcase.
- Don't get caught up in warranties. Most protect against manufacturer defects, not usage.
- We think a bag that can expand out is an absolute must-
have feature. Because you just never know what items you'll
pick up in your travels.

PERSONAL FLOTATION DEVICES (PFDs)

- Fit is paramount. It should fit snugly without impeding movement.
- Look for PFDs that are tested by Underwriters Laboratories
(UL) and approved by the U.S. Coast Guard. It should say so
on the label.

- Red, yellow, and orange PFDs are best for visibility. We suggest avoiding blue and green. (And we ask ourselves, why do they even make them in these hard-to-see colors?)
- Consider a sport-specific PFD. Kayaking PFDs have bigger armholes for ease of movement. Extra straps keep water-skiing vests on during wipeouts (not that we'd know).
- Once a PFD has been altered, its safety approval is no longer assured. So when buying used, avoid PFDs that have been patched, have badges or logos sewn on, or have been excessively written on. And check the Coast Guard's Web site (www.uscg.mil) for any recalls.
- PFDs with CO_2 cartridges inflate when you hit water. They're a great choice if you don't like the constriction of other vests. But be forewarned—they can inflate with even the slightest contact with water—like a sudden splash. And each time they inflate, you need to buy a replacement cartridge.
- Avoid buying used jackets made of kapok, which is found in some older PFDs. This is a natural fiber encased in plastic. If the plastic rips, the kapok takes on water, causing the jacket to act as an anchor, not a life preserver.

RUNNING SHOES

- Don't buy based on brand. Running is a high-impact activity, and you need a shoe that fits properly. Don't get caught up in the things like pumps, air, gel, or flashy designs either. Buy whatever shoe gives you the best support.
- Shop at a specialty store where a professional can fit you. Ill-fitting shoes can cause any number of serious joint and back problems.
- Before you buy, you need to know how your foot lands. One way to tell is to examine the bottom of an old shoe and see where the sole has worn away. If the sole has worn away evenly, you have a neutral foot; if it's worn along the instep, you pronate; and if it's worn along the outside edge, you supinate.

BONUS BAG:
Replace your old shoes about every three hundred to five hundred miles, or sooner if you see wear on the heel or rips in the lining.

- A neutral foot can wear almost any shoe and doesn't require specialized cushioning.
- If you pronate, you need a shoe with good motion control, firm support around the ankle, and a straight or semi-curved *last* (which simply refers to the overall shape of the shoe).
- If you supinate, you need a shoe with high arch support and a curved last. And check for flexibility on the inner side of the shoe.
- The shoe should feel comfortably snug. You should have about a half inch of space from your longest toe to the end of the shoe. (And in Anna's case, that's one very long toe.) Too loose, and there's not enough support and the potential for blisters. Too tight, and the foot can go numb.
- Don't buy shoes that need to be broken in. They should be comfortable right away.

HEART RATE MONITORS

We pitted portable heart rate monitors against professional ones doctors use. We found that chest models are generally more accurate than wrist-only models. We also found that with chest models, price is not an indicator of effectiveness. Look for ones with big faces that are easy to read and adjust when exercising. And while some users like seamless models that are more resistant to water or sweat damage, keep in mind you'll have to take them to a specialty shop when it's time to change the batteries.

- Avoid buying from stores where you can't return shoes after a few wears. If they're not comfortable, a reputable store that stands behind its products will let you exchange them for another model.
- Shop at the end of the day, when your feet are at their largest. And remember that often, you need a running shoe that's slightly larger than your regular shoe size.
- Look for a sole that's split in two to provide a smoother transition from heel to toe.
- We don't recommend buying online even if you've tried on that specific model elsewhere, as every pair of running shoes can fit a little differently.

SCOOTERS

- If you're looking for speed, make sure your scooter has continuously variable transmission, or CVT. Single-speed transmissions will let you go only about thirty miles per hour.
- If you're looking for power, go for a two-stroke engine. It burns both gas and oil—a powerful combination. A four-stroke engine, which burns only gas, is a more environmentally friendly choice.

- Four-stroke engines can overheat if driven for long periods or at high speeds, so consider how you'll use it.
- Disc brakes perform better than drum brakes, but they are more expensive.
- Pricier aluminum rims will last longer than steel rims.
- Bigger tires mean a smoother ride, while smaller ones provide better acceleration and control.
- Be sure to check out the storage capacity—you have to put those shopping bags somewhere!
- Test the kickstand. If you're a petite person, you may find some kickstands very difficult and cumbersome to use.

SKI AND SNOWBOARD HELMETS

- There are no federal safety standards for ski helmets, so make sure the helmet you're considering meets voluntary safety standards set by the European Committee for Standardization or ASTM International (American Society for Testing and Materials).
- Full-shell helmets give the most protection, as well as a little extra defense from the cold and wind.
- If you're using your helmet in warm conditions, consider a half-shell model, which will be better ventilated than the full shell. Plus you can usually remove the earflaps.
- Buy a helmet with vents to help cool you down when you're working up a sweat on the slopes.
- Earflaps will keep your ears toasty, but make sure they don't limit your ability to hear.
- Various brands fit differently, so try on several when shopping. A helmet should sit just above the eyebrows, not high on the

forehead. And it should be snug but not tight, or you'll get a headache. Hold it in place, and move your head from side to side. It should shift only slightly.

- Find out if the helmet you're considering has a replacement policy. Once you take a serious hit, some companies will replace your helmet at a fraction of the cost. (Even the best helmets suffer interior damage after a severe crash.)
- Take your goggles and sunglasses shopping with you to make sure they can work with the helmet.

SKIS–DOWNHILL

- The right ski for you depends on where you'll be using it. If you ski mainly in the East or in icy or hard-packed conditions, consider a carving ski. Powder or fat skis are ideal for the more powdery snow conditions in the West. If you ski in many types of conditions, an all-terrain or all-mountain ski is your best bet. Speed demons like Anna should opt for racing skis, while mogul junkies like Kristina should go for freestyle skis.
- Consider the flex. The softer or more flexible the ski, the easier it is to turn. You should be able to flatten the ski when standing on it. Beginners and women (who are generally lighter than men) will want a ski with more flex. The heavier or more advanced you are, the less flex you need.
- If you're a woman, we recommend buying skis designed for women. They are also lighter and easier to haul around. (It's very uncool to have your man carry your skis!)
- Consider the length. The ski should stand somewhere between your forehead and your nose. Beginners might want something shorter, as shorter skis are easier to maneuver.
- Check the side-cut. The more cut out or shaped the ski is, the easier it will be to turn. That said, absolute beginners

may find skis with a large side-cut more difficult to control.

- Wood-core skis are stronger and last longer, but are more expensive than foam-core skis. Foam is often used in women's skis because it is lighter. Make sure the foam is not *injected,* as that type of construction tends to break down sooner. Foam reinforced with fiberglass is a good bet.
- Skis reinforced with titanium or carbon give a smoother ride at higher speeds.
- Test-drive the skis. Shop at stores that will let you rent demo skis. If you buy them there, the rental fee should be deducted from the retail price. Manufacturers also often hold demo days right on the mountain.
- When buying used, make sure there aren't big gouges in the base and that the edges haven't started separating. And hold the skis base to base to check the camber—there should still be a space between the skis. If there's no space, the skis don't have much life left in them.
- For deals, shop at the end of the season, which is typically some-time in March. A low-snowfall year will often mean earlier sales.
- Don't forget to have your skis waxed and tuned regularly!

> When I get on a new ski, especially a different model, it will take me a few runs before I find that sweet spot and know how to work it well. You want to give a ski several runs before you can really find whether it's right for you or not. You want to feel a nice easy edge-to-edge switch, how they hold on to the snow. You want to look at the flex. Do they bounce around, or do they absorb the terrain?
>
> **–ROB BOYD,** FORMER OLYMPIC DOWNHILL SKIER AND THREE-TIME WORLD CUP CHAMPION

SLEEPING BAGS

- High-tech synthetic bags do a good job of keeping you warm. They are also cheaper, dry faster than down, and re-tain insulation even when wet. Plus, you can wash and dry them.
- Down bags are costlier but also lighter, warmer, and can be packed into a small, tight roll. With proper care, they can last a lifetime. They're best for hikers and those camping in

more extreme weather conditions. But if the bags get wet, they take forever to dry, so be sure to buy a cover if you go this route.

- The higher the fill of the down bag, the warmer it will keep you. Good bags are made with a fill power of around 600.
- We don't recommend cotton sleeping bags. They're useless when wet (not to mention heavy). Save them for indoor slumber parties.
- Sleeping bags come with a temperature or comfort rating. This indicates the lowest *outdoor* temperature the bag can keep you warm at. For example, a good-quality three-season bag (spring, summer, and fall) will have a temperature rating around 10 to 20 degrees F. If you'll be camping in temperatures lower than that, you'll need a thicker, winter sleeping bag.
- Bags come in three shapes: rectangular, semirectangular, and mummy. Choose a bag depending on how you sleep. (Mummy bags aren't good for claustrophobics!)
- Remember: You lose 50 percent of your body heat through your head. This makes a hood and a draft collar nice to have when the mercury goes south.
- Make sure the zippers glide easily all the way around the bag. And look for a draft tube behind the zipper, which will help seal out air and moisture.
- Don't buy a sleeping bag that's too big. It should fit snugly, otherwise all that warm air inside will escape. That means a child should have a child-size bag.

SHOPPING BAGS VERDICT: To test down and synthetic sleeping bags, we decided to spend a night under the stars in the outback—out back of Kristina's parents' house, that is. We slept straight through sunrise and awoke to the nasty glare of rolling cameras. (You should see what Anna's hair looks like in the morning!) For our summer sleepover, we preferred the synthetic sleeping bag—we found the down was too warm and got somewhat damp in the morning dew.

SNOWBOARDS

- A *free-ride* board is good for various conditions. A *freestyle* board is better for tricks and half pipes (leave that to the experts!)—they're shorter and lighter. *Free-carve* boards are longer and great for powder. *Race* boards are longer and stiffer and built for speed.
- Get a board that stands between your nose and your chin.
- Your weight is very important in determining the right board size. Heavy riders need more stiffness, while lighter riders require more flex. Width is also key, so be sure to stand on the board. Your feet should be near the edge without going over. This will give you optimum control.
- Check the side-cut. The more pronounced it is, the easier it will be to turn.
- Women may want to consider a women's board. They're narrower in size to accommodate smaller feet, and more flexible, which makes for easier maneuverability.
- Rent or demo first, especially when starting out. That will give you an idea of the type of riding you want to do. And rent the board from a store that will deduct the rental price if you decide to buy.
- Choose the right size board *before* you get enamored with graphics and colors. Cheaper boards tend to be heavier and bear simple graphics. High-end boards are often designed by pro riders and carry their signature. You'll pay more for an endorsed board.
- When buying used, check the sides of the board to ensure they're not separating. Smaller gouges in the base can be fixed; just make sure you negotiate a good deal.
- For cost savings, buy last year's models, and shop at the end of the season or in the summer, when boards are on sale.

> Used equipment is a wonderful thing. I wouldn't go back too many years, though. You want to know what year your equipment is. In this day and age, you can probably pick up your whole setup, bindings, board, and boots, for around five hundred or six hundred dollars.
>
> **—ROSS REBAGLIATI,**
> **THE FIRST OLYMPIC**
> **GOLD MEDALIST IN**
> **SNOWBOARDING**

SPORTS BRAS

- There are two kinds of sports bras: compression and encapsulation.
- Compression bras hold breasts firmly against the chest. They're better suited for A and B cups. Encapsulation or harness styles hold breasts in individual cups. This style is better for C cups and up.
- In general, the more fabric, the more support. But make sure you can move freely to avoid chafing.
- Stretch the fabric both horizontally and vertically. The bra needs to stretch horizontally so that you can pull it over your head. But if you are looking for more support, make sure the bra doesn't have too much vertical stretch.
- Thick straps offer more support. With encapsulation styles, look for adjustable straps. A racer back is good if your straps tend to fall down frequently.
- Look for a breathable fabric or a wicking fabric. Avoid all-cotton bras—they absorb perspiration and take forever to dry.
- Seams tend to show through on thin shirts, so watch out for styles that have seams running across the center of the breast pocket. We like bras with as few seams as possible.

TENNIS RACKETS

- Check the head size. Beginners should consider a larger-headed racket, as it makes it easier to hit the ball. Smaller heads require more skill and are good for those with powerful swings.
- Most rackets are made with aluminum, hyper carbon, or graphite. Generally, aluminum is inexpensive, hyper carbon is moderately priced and a good choice for beginners, and graphite is lighter, stiffer, and most durable. At the high end, titanium is extremely strong and light, and a good choice for committed players.
- Check the grip. When your hand wraps around, there should be a finger's width space between your fingers and the base of your thumb. Also, check the grip's material to ensure it will be easy to hold on to once you begin to sweat.
- Consider the racket's length and weight. Longer and heavier means more power, but such rackets are also more difficult to use.

- Every string has a particular gauge number, usually 15, 16, or 17. The higher the gauge number, the more spring you'll have, but you'll lose some durability. A beginner should go with thin-gauged string that's loosely strung.
- Synthetic gut strings are the best type of string for the average player. They're not as expensive as real gut, and they're more durable than nylon.
- Don't get caught up in the marketing lingo and high-tech labeling on many of today's rackets. You really need to demo a racket to determine whether it works for you. Should you buy it, the rental price is usually subtracted from the retail price. Ask before you rent.
- If you're looking for a deal, check out old demo rackets. Since they're used, you'll be able to get a better price.

TENTS

- The first question to ask yourself is this: Do you want something lightweight to take hiking? Or do you need something with lots of features and space for car camping?
  - Three-season tents are sufficient for most campers. But they don't hold up well under heavy snowfall.
  - How easy is it to set up? Some stores will let you set it up on the sales floor—you may feel silly doing it, but we highly recommend it!
  - Do a space test: Climb inside to check headroom and length, and visualize your gear in there, too. Remember that manufacturers measure capacity by how many people can lie side-by-side in the tent, and they don't factor in baggage.
  - Check the ventilation. Without it, you won't have a comfortable sleep.
  - Look for a covered entryway where you can store dirty shoes, gear, and the like.
  - Freestanding tents have more poles than tunnel tents, but we found them

SHOPPING BAGS VERDICT: We went on an overnight camping trip and barely made it out alive. No, it wasn't the bugs or the bears—it was the five tents we had to put up in hundred-degree heat. Let's just say we got a little grouchy after struggling with the eight-man "hotel." Our favorite was a dome tent by Coleman. It was roomy and fairly easy to assemble.

easier to set up and move. Tents with guylines can be tricky (as we found out on a sandy beach, with nowhere to stake things down).

- Aluminum poles are strong, light, and durable. Poles made of carbon fiber are lighter and stronger, but more expensive, too.
- Look for a ripstop nylon fabric that is polyurethane-coated to repel water. (It looks like little squares.) And check for taped seams, which give you extra protection against leaks.
- And here's a must for rainy weather: Look for a rain fly that *completely* covers the tent. When it rains, the water will drain off.

TREADMILLS

- Don't go cheap when buying your treadmill. If it isn't sturdy and it doesn't run smoothly, you won't use it. Also, you'll need a sturdier machine if you plan to run and not just walk.
- Check the motor size. Look for a minimum of *2 continuous horsepower.* Peak horsepower is not as important.
- Look for a deck that's shock absorbent. It should be at least ¾ to 1 inch thick, 20 inches wide, and 55 inches long. Make sure it doesn't wobble, and listen to the motor noise. If you find it loud in the store, imagine it competing with your television.
- Check the program options and display for ease of use. We like a good selection of programs to keep boredom at bay. And we don't like treadmills with hydraulic pistons—you can't change the incline while running.
- Make sure there is a safety feature for emergency stops.
- Bring your running shoes and test various models in the store. This is a must!
- Treadmills break down more than most other exercise machines. You'll want a good manufacturer's warranty included in the price. Look for *at least* five years on the motor (ten years is standard) and two years on parts. Also, buy from a specialty fitness store, rather than from a department store or box store, because they can deal with repairs if need be.
- You don't need a gym-quality treadmill. These models are heavy-duty because they take hours upon hours of abuse each day.

- We don't recommend buying a treadmill over the Web or through an infomercial. You really need to try out the equipment.

YOGA CLOTHES

- Choose a fabric that's stretchy, not slippery. Look for yoga clothes with at least 14 percent Lycra content. They'll move with your body.
- Look for a moisture-wicking fabric. Pure cotton does not dry quickly and can leave you cold, especially during that final "corpse" pose.
- Check the seams, and look for flat-lock stitching as opposed to serge stitching. Flat-lock stitching lies flat and causes less chafing.
- We suggest spending more on bottoms. You want a mid-weight fabric that can hold up to stretching and bending.
- Look for a fitted top, like camisoles with built-in bras. Loose T-shirts will fall over your head during inverted postures and leave you exposed!
- Avoid tops with plastic adjusters on the strap. They can dig into your back when you're lying down, and they tend to break easily.
- When trying on yoga clothes, assume some poses in the changing room. You want clothes that stay put and aren't fussy. Ommmm.

7. Bringing Up Baby: Kid Stuff

A new baby means you'll need a lot of new stuff—diapers, bibs, baby food, strollers, toys, and high chairs, just to name a few. It's estimated that a new baby will cost you about six thousand dollars in the first year alone! And as this child grows, new gear has to replace the old. Of course, you want to buy the very best you can afford to protect your most prized possession.

But what about buying for a friend's child when you don't have one of your own? We all have to attend a baby shower at some time or another, but how do you know what to buy when the closest you come to an infant is during your morning jog past the neighborhood day care? Parent or not, navigating your way through all the choices in the baby aisle is a challenge. Allow us to guide you through the maze of baby and kid stuff.

> The average North American baby will go through eight thousand diapers by the time he or she is toilet trained.

BABY SUPPLIES

The first place to start is the gift registry at your local department store or kids' store. Why buy when you can receive? Trust us—when you have a baby, everyone will want to give you something. So why not ensure that you get things you want and really need?

Whether you're registering or making the purchase yourself, there are a few major items you'll need before your bambino arrives. These include things like car seats, strollers, cribs, baby carriers, and high chairs. But before you go on a spending spree, ask yourself these questions:

1. DO I REALLY NEED IT?

Sure, a fancy changing table would be a nice addition to the baby room. But you can easily change the baby on the top of an appropriate dresser or on a changing pad that's placed on the floor or on a bed or couch.

2. CAN I BORROW IT?

Babies grow out of their clothes within three months. Most of the stuff you buy for your newborn will be in the garage collecting dust within three years (unless, of course, you have another baby). All this means it's an excellent time to put some thrifty measures into place. Any experienced parent will tell you that it's a good idea to borrow many essential items, particularly things like baby carriers and clothes. In fact, most of the mothers we've interviewed say they're always exchanging baby and kid stuff with their friends and siblings who have children older and younger than their own.

3. CAN WE BUY IT SECONDHAND?

While it is a great idea to shop for some baby and children's things secondhand, there are some items that prove the exception, or at least require an extremely detailed once-over, before you part with your money.

The Consumer Product Safety Commission discourages the use of used cribs and used car seats. But that's not to say you can't find safe products at a consignment store or through friends. Look for the certification seal of the Juvenile Products Manufacturers Association on all such products to ensure they meet national safety standards. Regulatory standards vary from country to country, and in some places, the rules may not be as strict as in the United States. So think twice before buying imported baby furniture, new or used.

TOY STORES

We say safety first. After that, we weigh cost against how long the toy is likely to remain of interest. When shopping *with* children, an early lesson in marketing can't hurt. Explain to children as young as five or six years old why they see commercials and how toy makers try to get kids to buy their toys. Talk to them about how companies create a need to buy lots of toys. This won't stop them from buying into the latest fads from time to time—don't we all?—but at least they can begin to understand it.

> The largest toys are often found on the bottom shelves and within easy reach of small hands. Smaller, less expensive figurines and dolls, and all their component parts, are found higher up.

When you walk into the store, think product placement. Major department stores like Wal-Mart and Toys "Я" Us typically put the latest and most advertised toys at the very back of the store. You and junior will have to pass by many other temptations before you get what you came for, and then pass by them all again on your way to the checkout. (A similar tactic to that used by grocery stores.)

We've noticed that the sections of educational toys are expanding all the time and becoming more inviting. These sections of the store are often carpeted, allowing kids and parents to sit down and thumb through books and learning materials that just aren't as immediately interactive as noisy monster trucks and talking dolls.

When your child has a particular toy in mind, help him or her evaluate it for both sturdiness and creative longevity—will it hold their interest beyond one play session? Learning toys are great, but kids can experience educational overload. Basic play is important, too. And here's a test to find out how badly they want the toy: Would they spend their own money? (A little dose of reality always helps!)

So whether it's time to go toy shopping or time to stock up on baby food, check out our tips on the following pages, and get the most for your shopping dollar.

HERE'S WHAT'S IN
OUR SHOPPING BAG

BABY CARRIERS

- Shopping for a carrier is a family affair. Look for adjustable straps if both parents are going to be using it (especially if you're a shrimp and your honey's a giant), and bring baby with you—you'll want to make sure they take to their new form of transport.

- Consider your lifestyle. Do you plan on taking your baby hiking? Do you live in an apartment? Take the bus? How big is your car? How old is your baby? These questions need to be answered before deciding what type of carrier you need and whether you need your carrier to work *with* a stroller or in place of a stroller.

- Front carriers are designed for newborns weighing between eight and twenty-five pounds, while back carriers are meant for older babies who can sit up, and for toddlers.

- Our testers found that slings are uncomfortable for long periods of time and best used around the house to soothe a cranky baby or on short shopping trips.

- If you do buy a sling, make sure it has adjustable straps held by nonslip rings or buckles.

- In a front carrier, look for one that's machine washable, that has straps and clasps that can be operated with one hand, and that opens on both sides for added convenience.

- In a back carrier, look for padded shoulder straps, a safety belt to prevent a squirming baby from falling out, and a heavy-duty frame if you plan on going on long hikes (or treacherous shopping expeditions!).

- A freestanding carrier stands up on its own when you set it on the ground, making it much easier to lift baby in and out.

- Make sure leg holes on front carriers aren't too big. (Believe it or not, there have been cases of newborns slipping out of their carriers.)

FAST FACT: Most people can comfortably carry a baby that weighs up to a quarter of their own weight.

- Know when to say when. If it hurts your back to pick up your baby, you might have a hard time putting on a back carrier with baby in it.
- Avoid buying used carriers unless they are from a trusted source—some models have been recalled for safety reasons.

BABY FOOD

- Watch out for added starches and sugars. Ingredients like flour or modified starch will only dilute food and fill your baby up without providing any extra nutrients.
- Choose foods that are fortified with iron—especially for infants aged six to twelve months who are being weaned off iron-rich breast milk. A common misconception is that "extra" iron will cause constipation problems. Not so. The iron fortification is often just the amount that's needed. Consult your pediatrician.
- Choose single foods rather than mixed dinners. A jar of strained carrots plus a jar of chicken offers better nutrition for your dollar than a single jar of chicken-vegetable dinner.
- When buying a single fruit, vegetable, or meat product, select the brand with the most calories, hence the most food per unit weight.
- Avoid "toddler foods." Baby-food companies continually seek ways to expand their sales base, and some have foods specifically for toddlers. But toddlers can easily chew and swallow small portions of most adult foods.
- Don't forget to check the expiration date.

BABY MONITORS

- Look for monitors that come with a light indicator as well as an audio indicator—that way you can still use it even when there are other sounds in the home (like a vacuum cleaner).
- Check the range posted on the box, but remember that it is measured in open, unobstructed space and doesn't necessarily take walls and stairways into account. Reception will definitely vary.
- Some monitors have two channels (like on a cordless phone). That way you can switch between them if you experience interference.
- Look for a model that gives you the option of using a plug or batteries. That way you can be efficient at night and plug it

in, but during the day you have the convenience of carrying it with you as you move around the house.

- Unless you really want to watch your baby by remote control, we think that baby monitors that come with a video component are just too expensive.
- Got a neighbor with a baby? Try to buy a different model of monitor. If you have the same one, you could wind up hearing their conversations and, more important, they could hear yours.
- We like models with indicators telling you when the battery is low or when you're out of range.

BIKES–KIDS (TWO-WHEELERS)

- A combination of hand brakes and pedal brakes offer the best safety. Keep in mind that some smaller kids (who don't have as much strength) find hand brakes too difficult to operate.
- Look for cantilever brakes. They're sturdier than side-pull brakes because they're attached to the frame in two places.
- Look for aluminum rims on the wheels. They're easier for the brakes to grab on to than chrome-plated steel rims, which can be slippery.
- A steel frame is sturdier than aluminum, but also heavier. Something to consider if you'll be the one lifting the bike in and out of the trunk.
- Be sure to get the right size. There should be about one inch of space above the crossbar and your child. And remember, anything too big is a safety hazard. A bike isn't something your child should grow into.
- A used bike can be a good option. But ensure there is no rust on the brake cables. (Rust on the chain is easy to get off.) And make sure the pedals spin smoothly. If they're making any strange sounds, it could indicate a problem with the

bearings, which can be expensive to fix.

- Don't forget to budget for a helmet and a light!

BUILDING TOYS

- The construction toy should match the child's age and ability. A construction set that's too advanced can lead to frustration. And big heavy blocks might not be best for a child who likes to throw things.
- Before you buy, ensure that the blocks fit together easily, and look for a variety of pieces to give your child lots of building options.
- *Unit blocks* are so called because the smaller blocks are an eighth, one-half, or a quarter the size of the largest block in the set. They're usually made of wood and are therefore very durable. Our toy experts favor unit blocks because they help introduce kids to the concepts of mathematics and proportion.
- Watch for flimsy accessories that can break off. They can create sharp edges and become a choking hazard for younger children.
- Complicated themed sets are fun and challenging to put together, but we agree with our pint-size testers: Regular blocks that you can use again and again to build any number of things are best for optimizing creativity.
- When buying complex sets, check out the instructions. If you can't understand them, will your eight-year-old?
- How many blocks to buy? Our toy experts suggest two hundred blocks for a three-year-old, three hundred for a four-year-old, and four hundred for a five-year-old. (Can you imagine how many blocks we would need?)

SHOPPING BAGS VERDICT: After all the time we spent researching and considering what to look for in a bike for your child, we got a laugh out of our kid testers' final analysis. After spending weeks with the test bikes, the consensus was clear: They just wanted a bike in their favorite color! So don't forget to consider that, too.

CAR SEATS

- Before you shop for a seat, it's important to know the federal safety laws, as they ultimately determine what kind of car seat you need. Check the Web site of the National Highway Traffic Safety Administration (www.nhtsa.dot.gov).
- Infant seats are for a child from birth to twenty-two pounds and are strictly rear-facing.
- Convertible seats are designed to protect children from infancy to seat-beltage. They can hold children up to eighty pounds and can be rear- or forward-facing. Some even convert to a booster seat.

FAST FACT: Nearly one-third of children ride in the wrong constraints for their age and weight.

- A booster seat is for a child who weighs anywhere between forty and eighty pounds. They have a carry handle and are strictly forward-facing.
- Make sure the car seat you buy has been certified by the National Highway Traffic Safety Administration (NHTSA).
- A five-point harness is considered the safest way to strap in your baby.
- Look for padding on the seat that is both removable and washable.
- When buying for babies, get a car seat with a separate seat and base. That way you can snap baby out of the base, go about your business, and easily snap baby back in.
- Not all car seats fit in all cars. Be sure to take the seat out to your car and test it before you make the commitment to buy. And it's a good idea to take your car and car seat to a local car-seat-inspection site to ensure you're using it properly. Go to www.nhtsa.dot.gov for more information.
- When looking for car seats, you may see references to LATCH, which stands for Lower Anchors and Tethers for Children. This is a feature that's found on most cars made since 2002 that eliminates the need to use lap belts to secure the seat to your car—but you'll still need the tether strap when the seat is forward-facing. A LATCH system is not necessarily safer than the old seat-belt method, but it might make securing the seat easier. And of course, you'll still need to make sure the seat fits your car properly.

- Be careful about buying used car seats, as some models have been recalled. Check the NHTSA or the U.S. Consumer Product Safety Commission Web sites for product details.

COLORED MARKERS

- Safe markers will have either an AP (Approved Product) or a CP (Certified Product) logo on them. This means they've been approved by the Arts and Creative Materials Institute and are deemed nontoxic and nonhazardous.
- Smell the markers in the store. Stinky permanent markers could cause dizziness, nausea, and headaches if used in poorly ventilated places.
- Don't buy markers with caps that are smaller than three inches by three inches for children under four years old. They're a choking hazard.
- When shopping, check out the marker's nib. Broad nibs are better for big jobs, and they're easier for younger kids to control. Thin nibs are better for detail work.
- Don't worry too much about markers drying out. We left the caps off four different brands of markers for five days straight. Only the Crayola dried out; the Mr. Sketch, Laurentien, and Prang Classic Artist stayed moist.

SHOPPING BAGS VERDICT: During our tests, we learned that most nonpermanent markers will indeed come out of clothing, but they may not necessary come off your walls. Something to think about before leaving kids and markers unattended in your freshly painted living room.

CRIBS

- Always look for a clearly labeled make or model number on the crib you're considering, as manufacturers will relay this information in the event of a recall. Don't see it? Don't buy it.
- Safety standards on cribs changed in 1986, so if you're hoping to use that family heirloom or buy used, be sure to examine the distance between the rails or slats. If a soda can fits through them, so could a baby's head. And watch out for cribs with posts or knobs on the head or footboard—active toddlers can easily hook their clothing on them.

- We recommend coil mattresses as opposed to foam—they're stronger and offer more support. Look for one that's firm and fits snugly against the sides—gaps wider than two fingers could trap limbs and be potentially unsafe. And check for soft spots on any used mattresses—they can be a suffocation hazard.

- Cribs with wheels make picking up stray toys and changing linens easier. Wheels equipped with a locking mechanism provide added stability.

- We like drop-down sides that can be adjusted with one hand. They allow you to lower the side while putting your sleepy infant to bed. That said, double-drop-sided cribs aren't that useful, since most people put one side of the crib up against a wall.

- Cribs that convert to toddler beds or even twin beds may be a good option for those planning on only one child. But they are pricey. Buying a crib and toddler bed separately is often more economical, so be sure to compare prices.

- Check underneath the crib to make sure the mattress support is made from metal. You shouldn't be able to adjust the height without using tools.

DIAPERS

- Decide whether you're going to go with disposable diapers or cloth. There is no question that cloth is the more environmentally friendly and economical choice. But disposable diapers are miles ahead when it comes to convenience and absorbency.

- Look for disposables with resealable tabs. They'll save you time and money when checking for wetness. (This is also a good feature when you have to fix those poor diapering jobs by inexperienced but well-meaning relatives!)

- The right fit is crucial when choosing a diaper. Otherwise you'll be dealing with messy leaks and an unhappy baby. Be sure to check the weight and height guidelines on the outside of the package. Cloth diapers are typically easy to adjust for size, but it is still something to inquire about with your supplier.

- While disposable diapers are becoming more absorbent all the time, our experts still recommend changing them as often as you would cloth (three to four hours). This frequency will prevent bacteria from accumulating and removes the moisture that can cause diaper rashes.

- Some companies have come out with boy- and girl-specific diapers, arguing they better target areas where urine accumulates with boys (the front) and girls (the middle to back). But the pediatricians we asked say the suggested urine gender difference is minor—if it exists at all—so there's no need to make this part of your diaper-selection criteria.

- If you're going with cloth diapers, keep in mind that terry cloth is one of the most absorbent options. It's also more durable than flannel. But it does tend to be bulky, which can make double-diapering at night difficult.

SHOPPING BAGS VERDICT: In our tests, brand-name disposables out-performed generic brands when it came to absorbency. The Huggies diaper came in first, followed closely by the Pampers. However, we also found that the big brand names didn't necessarily fit better than the generics, so the deciding vote may ultimately go to your baby.

HIGH CHAIRS

- Look for the seal of the Juvenile Products Manufacturers Association (JPMA), a trade organization of more than four hundred companies in the United States, Canada, and Mexico. The seal indicates the chair meets voluntary safety standards set by ASTM International (American Society for Testing Materials).

- Plastic chairs are lighter and often come with more features than metal ones.

- Look for a one-handed tray release—you'll probably have baby in the other!

- A high chair with wheels will make repositioning easier.

SHOPPING BAGS VERDICT: The parents and day-care workers who helped us test several high chairs chose the Peg Perego chair as their favorite because of its five-point harness, reclining seat, one-handed tray removal, and ability to fold away.

- Wait until you actually need the chair before buying it. That way you'll have a better idea of what fits your baby best.
- Vinyl seats are the easiest to clean, but if you prefer fabric, make sure it's removable so it can be washed.
- Old-fashioned wooden chairs may look nice, but they are often difficult to adjust to fit your baby perfectly.
- A reclining seat is convenient for a baby who likes to nap after a meal, but don't feed your baby in the reclined position.
- Run your hands over the edges of the seat to ensure that nothing is sharp or protruding.

JUNGLE GYMS

- A backyard jungle gym made from wood is sturdier than one made from metal or plastic. Cedar or redwood are good choices.
- Avoid pressure-treated wood. It contains chemicals like copper chromium arsenate (CCA), creosote, or pentachlorophenol (or all), which are all potential carcinogens. As of January 2004, CCA can no longer be used to treat wood used in residential settings, so if you are buying a new gym, you'll be fine. If you're buying a used jungle gym—something we don't recommend—check the manufacturing dates.
- It's important your jungle gym is placed on a deep, soft surface to help cushion falls. Grass and dirt are *not* recommended. Pea gravel, sand, shredded bark mulch, wood chips, or rubber matting are safer choices.
- Shop according to the age of your kids. Most sets are built to suit a particular age range, typically either two to five years, or five to twelve.
- If you're not that handy with tools, inquire about an assembly service when you shop. Assembling jungle gyms can range from the straightforward to a major weekend chore!
- There are many components to choose from. Take your kids to a local playground, and watch which

BONUS BAG: Face slides to the north if possible. If they face south, the sun can heat them up, and that can mean a burned bottom!

type they prefer. Research shows boys tend to prefer climbing, and girls like slides.

- When installing railings, make sure they're vertical. Anything horizontal looks like a ladder, and you can bet kids will climb it! Also make sure railings are close enough together that a child's head couldn't get stuck.

PLAYPENS

- Make sure the playpen you're considering has been approved by the Juvenile Products Manufacturers Association (JPMA). This means it has met the rigorous safety standards of the American Society for Testing Materials.
- If you're buying secondhand, choose a model manufactured after 2000. (Safety standards on playpens were significantly revised in the early part of that year, following a rash of product recalls.) Also check that the playpen hasn't been repaired or altered in any way, as its safety approval may no longer be assured.
- Look for a playpen that has a double-locking mechanism on each arm (most newer ones do) to prevent the structure from collapsing.
- Examine how the playpen is put together: Seams and edges should lie flat, so there's nothing the baby could step on to climb out; mesh walls should be lightly stretched, provide good ventilation, and allow you to see the baby clearly.
- Floor pads should be a maximum of one inch thick and fit snugly against the edge of the playpen. Check it for firmness, not softness. Something that cushions too much could be a suffocation hazard.
- Be sure to carry around and erect the playpen in the store before you buy. Some are very cumbersome—an important consideration if you're taking both the playpen and baby over to grandma's.
- Don't get caught up in extra features you and your little one don't need. We found

HEALTH ALERT:
Playpens are not recommended for children weighing more than thirty to thirty-five pounds. At that weight, they're strong enough to hoist themselves out.

add-ons, like bassinets and changing tables, weren't worth the extra weight. In fact, the simplest playpen, the Evenflo Roll n' Go, was our overall favorite.

STROLLERS

- Look for a five-point harness to keep the baby securely strapped in. Brakes provide added safety.
- Lightweight "umbrella" strollers are easy to maneuver and inexpensive. But they also aren't the most durable or comfortable.
- Old-fashioned carriage strollers can be heavy and difficult to push uphill.
- Many parents love car-seat strollers, where the car seat snaps into the stroller base. That way you don't have to wake up baby when making a move. Of course, babies outgrow this type of stroller quickly. For this reason, we prefer regular upright strollers that can be reclined for sleeping.
- Consider where you'll use the stroller. If you plan to go on gravel or if you're going to jog, go for a jogging stroller with thick rubber wheels. A front wheel that swivels provides optimum maneuverability.
- Double strollers that sit side by side are very difficult to get through shop doors.
- Tipping is the most common source of stroller injuries, so look for a wheelbase that's wide and sturdy. And check the location of the storage compartment. It should be located low down so heavy items can't tip the stroller.
- Check that the fabric is washable and offers your baby good insulation. Some models will need lots of additional blankets to keep baby warm in winter.
- Ensure the canopy is big enough to shield the entire seat from sun and rain.

As a mom of two young kids, I'm familiar with a lot of baby gear. When it comes to strollers, I look for great style and features for both myself and my daughter. I look for the single-hand fold, and the comfort aspect of the handles. Maclaren's Techno Classic Stroller is a great choice. It's what I use, and I'd highly recommend it for new parents.

–JOSIE BISSETT,
ACTOR

- Test-drive the stroller around the store. If it's collapsible, is it easily done? And does it fit in your trunk?
- Strollers often face product recalls. If you're buying or receiving a secondhand stroller, be sure to check the Consumer Protection Safety Commission Web site for any product alerts (www.cpsc.gov).

8. Odds and Ends: Home Maintenance Essentials

Lightbulbs, lint brushes, and toilet paper? You call this shopping? You bet! These are the sorts of items we need to keep our homes running smoothly. It's stuff we wish we didn't have to drop dollars on, but the good news is there are ways to spend less.

GENERIC VERSUS NAME BRAND

Ever find yourself standing in the aisles at the grocery store or drugstore, pondering whether to buy the name-brand laundry detergent or the generic brand? Will Tide really get your clothes that much whiter?

> Simplify. You don't need a different cleaner or cleaning gizmo for every job. Ordinary dish soap is great on windows, baking soda makes toilet bowls sparkle, and a stiff toothbrush makes a mean scrubber (and gets in all those hard-to-reach areas—it was designed to!).

Tide, Windex, Kleenex, and the like have spent millions on making sure they are the most recognizable names on the shelf. And, as with packaged food manufacturers, these companies are continually coming out with new products (mountain scent, fresh scent, scent free!) to take up even more shelf space, catch your eye, and, hopefully, nab your dollar.

Think twice before you pay for the name. Many brand-name manufacturers also produce generic brands (store brands) right out of the same factories. Film is a great example. The next time you buy a generic brand, check the negatives. While the brand name is not printed on the box, if you hold the negative up to the light, you will see which major brand (Fuji, Kodak, and so on) manufactured it.

In our tests of common household goods, we found that paying more doesn't mean the product will perform better or last longer. When it comes to products like batteries and lightbulbs, generics often *outlasted* brand names. (Just remember that when buying batteries and film, you need to check the expiration date.) And keep in mind there aren't many "secret" ingredients on the market. For example, generic or not, the most common ingredient in glass cleaners is ammonia.

> If you're hiring a contractor to do some home renos, avoid working on a cash basis. Signing a contract puts the law on your side should anything go wrong.

BUYING GREEN

Many household maintenance products create a lot of waste. Chemical concoctions are constantly being flushed down the drain. Paper products and packaging are piling up in our landfills. To deal with this growing concern, there are an increasing number of environmentally friendly products available to consumers. They're made with less toxic materials or, in the case of paper products, with recycled goods.

We are firm believers in protecting the environment and buying products that are safe for both our families and our surroundings. But there is one important caveat: In general, we have found that "green" products, especially cleaning supplies, don't work as well as their "chemical" counterparts. So keep in mind that it may take a little more elbow grease or a little more product (and therefore money) to get the job done. And, really, do you have to have the whitest towels on the block? Here's a compromise: Use the green products for everyday jobs and the chemical-laden ones for the real heavy-duty (occasional) clean.

NEW DOESN'T ALWAYS MEAN IMPROVED

Every day, fancy new household gadgets appear on the market, designed to make your chores easier—things like battery-operated mops, or wipes for cleaning the microwave. And have you seen those dryer balls advertised on TV? Save your money, and throw in a tennis ball instead! (See the Bonus Bag on page 213 for more details.)

Before you go out and spend the big bucks on the latest and greatest, our tests show that simple models often work just as well as fancy, cutting-edge, pricey products, and even better in some cases. A waiter's corkscrew is more efficient than many high-end lever-types, which tend to break down; basic sponge mops and deck mops can reach those nooks and crannies better than disposable wet mops; and gizmos that promise to help you fold your clothes faster? Do you really need to ask?

Of course, in shopping, as in life, there are exceptions to every rule—be sure to read up on specific items in the section ahead to keep your home running like a well-oiled machine.

HERE'S WHAT'S IN OUR SHOPPING BAG

BATHROOM SCALES

- The least-expensive type of scale is the analog or mechanical scale. It's durable, but it does need resetting from time to time.
- Digital scales tend to be more accurate, but they can break down more often than mechanical scales. They also require a battery, so calculate that into the price.
- We prefer mechanical scales to digital for the price point. We also don't like the added expense and hassle of having to change those batteries.
- If you're watching your weight very closely, and want to monitor every single half-pound change, digital is the way to go.
- Body-fat scales measure your body mass index (a calculation of your weight and your percentage of body fat) by

sending a harmless electrical current through your body. These scales are expensive, and our experts recommend simply asking your doctor for a BMI test during your regular checkup. People with pacemakers should not use these scales.

- Look for a clear display with numbers large enough to read from a distance.
- Rubber feet or pads will help a scale stay in place, especially on a tiled floor.

BATTERIES

- *Heavy-duty* or zinc chloride batteries are good for low-energy-draining devices like alarm clocks and remote controls.
- Alkaline is the most common type of battery. They have about a seven-year shelf life and are good for items that sit unused for a long time, like a flashlight. Be sure to check the "stale date" or best-before date on the package (especially if it's on sale).
- When buying alkaline batteries, buy according to price, not brand. In our tests, brand names did not consistently outperform the no-name variety.
- Lithium batteries are very powerful and have a shelf life of ten years. They're used in equipment like digital cameras and high-tech devices. But they're expensive.
- Rechargeable batteries are a good choice if you want to be environmentally friendly. Plus, they can save you money in the long run. (But you shouldn't use these for items that sit idle for long periods, or the power will drain.)
- When buying rechargeables, check the milliamp hour (mAh). The higher the mAh, the longer the battery will last both in the long term and in between charges.
- Nickel-cadmium is the most inexpensive type of rechargeable battery. But it doesn't last forever. Most can be recharged between three hundred and five hundred times. These batteries also have a *memory effect.* Meaning, frequently recharging when the battery hasn't completely drained can significantly reduce their "live" time. Because of this defect, most major manufacturers have stopped making them.

- Nickel-metal hydrate is a higher-performance rechargeable and the most common. It does not have the "memory effect" and can be recharged three hundred to five hundred times.
- Lithium-ion is the superior type of rechargeable and is typically used in items that require a lot of power, like camcorders and cell phones. They can be recharged thousands of times.

CAR WAX

- Buy a car wax made with natural ingredients over waxes that are purely synthetic. Carnauba is a great natural wax that creates a longer-lasting shine.
- Go for a hard paste wax, which will have a higher concentration of carnauba.
- If you can, feel the texture of the wax at the store. Avoid anything that feels gritty.
- Avoid products that promise to wash and wax in one step. They generally wear off in three or four washings.
- If your car is dark colored, look for a wax specifically designed for dark cars. These waxes contain fewer abrasives, especially important for dark-colored vehicles.

CARPET SPOT CLEANERS

- Different cleaners work best on different types of carpets. Find out whether your carpet is made from wool or synthetic fibers, and make sure the cleaner is safe for those fibers. You may want to test the product in an obscure area, like the back of a closet.
- Don't expect one cleaner to work on all types of stains. You might need to have a few different kinds in your cleaning supply cupboard.
- Don't buy a cleaner that feels sticky. The leftover residue can attract dirt and

BONUS BAG: To find out whether your carpet is made from natural or synthetic fibers, cut a few strands from an inconspicuous area, and light it on fire—carefully! Wool will char, and synthetic will melt.

dust and, over time, create dark spots on your carpet. Talk about doing more harm than good.

- Check your carpet warranty, as some become void if you use the wrong type of cleaner.
- Most all-purpose brand-name cleaners contain chlorinated solvents, which are very toxic and carcinogenic. You often won't see ingredients on the label, because they're considered proprietary information. Spray a bit out in the store. If the smell is strong, it probably contains some of these toxic chemicals.
- If you do utilize these products, be sure to wear gloves and use them only in a well-ventilated area. Don't put children, especially toddlers, on a recently spot-cleaned carpet.
- We prefer nontoxic cleaners—they'll be labeled as such. In our tests, they performed as well as other major brands, and they're better for you and the environment.

DISH SOAP

- For regular everyday dishes, one dish soap is as effective as the next, so buy whatever's cheapest.
- If the scent of your dish soap matters to you, you're living in the era of choice! You'll spend ages in the soap aisle considering whether you want to be reminded of green apples or sea breezes while slaving away at the kitchen sink.
- If you want to take the environmentally friendly route, buy dish soap made from vegetable or plant-based oil as opposed to petroleum-based oil. You'll pay a bit more, but you'll also help conserve the Earth's depleting oil supply.
- Many dish soaps come in an *ultra* version, which is concentrated, so you don't need to use as much. But these soaps generally cost more per bottle, so make sure you do in fact use less each time, or it'll end up costing you more in the long run.
- Don't trust a label that claims to be *hypoallergenic*. The FDA doesn't regulate the use of this word, so any manufacturer can put it on a product without having to substantiate the claim.

DRAIN CLEANERS

- In our tests, products with sulfuric acid worked best. They literally eat through clogs. However, acids are very hard on your pipes and on the environment.

- Products containing bases (like sodium hydroxide or copper sulfide) are gentler but not as effective as acids.
- Aluminum flecks are added to some nonacidic drain cleaners to increase the heat of the chemical reaction and essentially dissolve stubborn clogs. But they can create buildup in pipes and actually make clogs worse. We don't recommend them.

SHOPPING BAGS VERDICT: Ever hear the urban myth that suggests pouring cola down your drain can unclog your pipes? Well, we tried it and it doesn't work. Save your cola for drinking instead.

- We found products from specialty plumbing stores more efficient than regular brand-name products. But they should be used sparingly and infrequently to avoid pipe damage.
- A mix of vinegar and baking soda is a cost-effective and safe option for small clogs. (Pour some in, and cover the drain. After a few minutes, rinse with boiling water.)

FABRIC SOFTENERS

- Manufacturers argue that liquids are better for softness, while sheets do a better job of combating static cling. While we agree that fabric softeners in general do the job, our tests did not reveal a big difference between liquids and sheets or from one brand to the next. We say, buy whatever's on sale.
- In terms of convenience, we prefer sheets. Liquid often has to be added at the right time during the wash cycle, whereas softening sheets can simply be thrown in the dryer.
- Use fabric softeners in limited doses. They all contain petroleum distillates and harsh chemical scents like

BONUS BAG: Here's an unusual type of fabric softener: When drying down-filled pillows, sleeping bags, or jackets, throw a couple of clean tennis balls into the dryer with them! They'll fluff up the down, break up any clumps, and reduce static cling.

benzyl acetate or limonene, which can cause allergic reactions and other health problems. (Make sure you do your laundry in a well-ventilated area and that the dryer duct vents outside. Otherwise, the moist dryer air creates ideal conditions for mold and insect mites.)

- Consider a nontoxic fabric softener. They're usually available only in liquid form, and use plant or citrus oils instead of petroleum-based compounds. Look for ones that biodegrade quickly (thirty days or less is good) and that are phosphate free.

- Use fabric softener sparingly on towels, as it will reduce their absorbency over time.

FILM

- The smaller the ISO number, the slower the film, and the more light a camera needs to take a clear picture. Higher-speed film costs more.

- Film speed can affect the graininess of the printed photo. In general, the faster the film the more grain there will be in the images. The slower the film, the sharper the image.

- Many photographers and film developers recommend a 400 ISO film for standard prints. We agree—this is a good all-purpose choice. But if you want to experiment, take some close-up pictures (preferably something with both smooth and rough edges) with the end of a 400 roll, and then immediately change to a 200 ISO roll and take the exact same shots. Don't forget to label your prints when they come back so you know which is which!

SHOPPING BAG VERDICT: Our tests revealed very little difference in color and contrast from one brand of film to the next. For everyday photography, go for the cheapest brand.

- Wondering about that supermarket brand? Our photography experts say these brands are usually manufactured by one of the big labels anyway, like Kodak or Fuji, and they take perfectly good pictures. You can find out which one by holding the film up to the light. The name is printed along the side.

- Establish a good relationship with your film developer—they play a big role in the quality and look of your photos.

FIRE EXTINGUISHERS

- Before you buy a fire extinguisher, you've got to know your ABCs. An extinguisher marked *A* will handle ordinary combustibles like wood and paper. A *B* extinguisher handles grease fires and other flammable liquids, and a product labeled *C* will attack electrical fires involving appliances or computers.

- For maximum protection, buy an all-inclusive A-B-C fire extinguisher. Using the wrong type could actually make a fire bigger.

- Look for the UL seal of approval. That means the extinguisher has been tested and certified by Underwriters Laboratories, Inc.—an independent, not-for-profit product safety-testing organization that is internationally recognized.

- Indoor fires double in size approximately every thirty seconds. A fire extinguisher is good for only eight to twenty-five seconds. Bottom line: Buy a *large* extinguisher. The bigger it is, the better your chance of putting out the flames. We recommend ones that are at least five pounds.

- A fire extinguisher is good only if you can get to it when you need it. Don't stop at just one—buy several, and ask for a discount for buying in bulk. The fire department recommends placing one every six hundred square feet, or one extinguisher per floor.

- Look for an expiration date. No one needs a stale fire extinguisher in the heat of the moment.

- A gauge is a good feature. It tells you whether the extinguisher has been discharged or if the pressure is low.

FIRE LOGS

- If you light a lot of fires, commercially manufactured fire logs are a good choice. They burn with less smoke and lower particulate and carbon monoxide emissions than regular wood.

- Some fire logs require you to cut a slit along one side of the package. Other types call for lighting on either end only with no requirement for making the slit. With these logs, lighting your fire becomes that much more convenient.

- Don't buy fire logs made from coffee beans for the supposed scent they give off. Our testers couldn't smell a thing.

- Some fire logs mimic the crackling sound you get from regular wood. But don't bother paying extra for logs with this feature. The sound is too faint to sound authentic, so any crackling you hear will be drowned out by conversation or music.

- If you use a wood stove, buy fire logs made with sawdust only. The ones made with wax burn hotter and can produce a blaze too hot for some stoves. It could create a fire hazard.
- Some fire logs contain chemicals that clean your chimney while they burn. But they usually cost two or three times the price of regular fire logs, and they do not eliminate the need to have your chimney professionally cleaned periodically. So think twice about spending the extra money.

GARBAGE BAGS

- If you never overstuff your garbage bags, go with generic brands. After all, you're only throwing them away.
- For a busy household that is hard on its trash, we like brand-name bags. Lab tests and our own real-life experiments all showed that they have more give than generic bags. You can pack more into them and, ultimately, use fewer bags.
- Environmentally friendly bags are another option. They're usually made with a higher percentage of recycled materials, and some biodegrade faster than traditional bags. These benefits duly noted, it's more important to reduce the garbage itself!

- We don't think it's worth it to spend more on bags with special ties and tabs. Save money by just going with simple twist ties or simply tie the corners of the bags together.

GLASS CLEANERS

- We don't recommend the premoistened glass cleaner towels. They're expensive, oversaturated with product (which means they'll streak), and they dry out if you're not diligent about keeping them tightly sealed.
- Avoid using all-purpose cleaners on glass. They tend to streak.
- Most glass cleaners on the shelves contain ammonia. If you want an ammonia product but also want to save money, go with a generic. They work just as well.
- After cleaning dozens of windows (and you thought our jobs were glamorous), we got the best results with ammonia-free products.
- Many glass cleaners put CONTAINS NO PHOSPHORUS on the label. But keep in mind this is standard in most any glass cleaner whether or not it is advertised.

SHOPPING BAGS VERDICT: Instead of buying glass cleaner, consider investing in a sponge, a squeegee, and dish soap. How do we know? We went thirty stories up and polled the guys who clean skyscraper windows for a living! This is what they use on windows at work and at home.

KITCHEN KNIVES

- The average cook needs only three knives: a chef's knife, a serrated knife (or bread knife), and a paring knife. The rest is gravy.
- Spend the most on your chef's knife. It can tackle 75 percent of the cutting jobs in the kitchen.
- Knife starter sets usually cost 25 percent less than if you buy all the knives separately.
- Look for high-carbon stainless steel. The higher the carbon content, the better it will hold an edge and the less it will rust.
- Check the knife's balance. It should balance at the point between the handle and the blade. While in the store, hold the knife against a flat surface and pretend to chop. Make sure the design gives you enough clearance so that you don't bang your knuckles on the table.

- Look for a full *tang*—this means the metal extends through to the end of the handle. A full tang means a strong knife. That said, if you have small hands or arthritis, or simply prefer a lighter knife, you can buy a good quality knife with a three-quarter tang.
- Synthetic handles last longer and are considered more hygienic than wood.
- The best knives are *taper ground*—this means the whole blade gradually tapers down to a sharp V. With hollow-ground knives, you'll see that only a small bottom portion is ground into an edge.

BONUS BAG: If you keep your knives in a wooden block, store them blade side up. This way you won't dull the blade as you pull them in and out.

LAUNDRY DETERGENT

- If you're looking to protect your clothes, go with a liquid detergent. It's gentler than a powder.
- Powders do a better job on heavy grime and nasty odors. They're usually cheaper than liquids, too. So if you have a household full of dirty kids, or if you play a lot of outdoor sports, they may be your best, most economical bet.
- Breaking out in a rash? Stay away from fragranced detergents. They are a common source of skin irritation. (Just ask Kristina.) Still sensitive? Trying limiting your use of detergents containing enzymes. They're effective at breaking down tough stains, but they can aggravate allergies. Save them for fabrics that need a heavy-duty cleaning.
- "Natural" detergents are better for the environment, but our tests showed that they aren't as good at cleaning clothes as regular brands. They also tend to cost more, so if you go this route, be sure you're getting the most environmentally friendly product available. Look for vegetable-based detergents that are nontoxic, biodegradable, and chlorine and phosphate free.

SHOPPING BAGS VERDICT: After washing piles and piles of laundry, we found that name brands worked a bit better than generics.

- National brands continually come out with new formulations and fragrances, but often this is just a tactic to take up more supermarket shelf space.
- When it comes to hand-washing delicate garments, shampoo is a good alternative to laundry detergent.

LAWN MOWERS

- Manual-reel mowers are economical, quiet, and environmentally friendly. Because they're entirely people powered, they're best suited to small, flat lawns or for those in search of exercise. They can't tackle seriously overgrown lawns, but they're fine for light day-to-day maintenance. (Kristina has one for her pint-size yard.)
- Electric mowers are quieter and more environmentally friendly than gas mowers. Because they need to be plugged in, they're best for smaller lawns and for homes with easy access to power outlets.
- Gas mowers are more powerful and convenient (no cord to flip around) and generally cut a larger swath than other types of mowers, reducing your mowing time slightly. But they're noisy, require more maintenance than electric mowers, and most important, are heavy polluters.
- If you do opt for a gas mower, choose one with a four-stroke engine. They're more fuel efficient and are recommended by the Environmental Protection Agency.
- Don't get carried away with horsepower. A five-horsepower engine is all the average homeowner needs.
- Bagged mowers store the clippings and produce a cleaner-looking lawn. But we like mulching mowers—it's better for your lawn, as the nutrients are returned to the ground, and there's nothing to throw away.
- Self-propelling mowers are very easy to push around and therefore a good choice for the elderly or those wishing to make mowing easier. (And then there's Anna. She doesn't like to mow the lawn at all!)
- Get a mower with a height adjustment—this makes it easier to cut long grass.

FAST FACT: A well-maintained lawn can add between 5 and 7 percent to the value of your home. Get mowing!

LIGHTBULBS

- An incandescent (regular) lightbulb is cheap to buy but expensive to run. It converts only about 10 percent of its energy into light. The rest is turned into heat.

- A halogen bulb will last longer, but it converts only 15 percent of its energy into light. It also gets very hot, so make sure it has lots of open space around it to reduce the fire hazard.

- We like compact fluorescent bulbs best. While they cost more to buy initially, they last eight times longer and use 75 percent less energy to run than an incandescent.

- When shopping for new bulbs, bring the old one with you. It can save you a lot of frustration when it comes to finding the right size and fit.

SHOPPING BAGS VERDICT: We tested six incandescent bulbs—two generic, two midprice, and two high end—to see if they'd last as long as promised on the package. Several weeks and many blackened bulbs later, the results were in. All the bulbs burned out earlier than promised! And while the brand-name bulbs lasted slightly longer than the generics, the difference in burning time was too slight to justify the much higher price. So when buying incandescents, think "no name."

MOPS

- *Deck mops* are made of yarn. Look for looped threads rather than cut ends. They're less likely to fray.

- Make sure your deck mop or cloth mop is machine washable. It will last longer if you can keep it clean.

- Sponge mops don't leave lint behind, and their heads dry faster, so there's less chance of mildew setting in.

- Watch for abrasive scratch pads attached to some sponge mops—they can scratch hardwood floors.

- Check the wringing mechanism of the sponge mop to ensure that it's easy to reach and use.

- Some wet mops are battery powered. We find these expensive to buy and maintain—you'll need to keep purchasing the disposable cloths, special cleaning solution, and batteries. Plus, they're not the best at cleaning corners or tackling grout. We don't think they're worth it.

- If you have lots of nooks and crannies in your home, go for a cloth mop. They're the best mop for cleaning hard-to-reach places and are well priced.
- Our overall favorites are sponge mops and cloth mops, but it depends on the job you're tackling. The nice part is that both kinds are inexpensive, so who's to say you can't have both?

MULTITOOLS (I.E., SWISS ARMY KNIVES)

- Determine your needs, and don't be oversold on features you'll never use. Most tools are used on hiking trips, so will you really need a wire cutter? An awl for cutting holes in belts? More than one saw blade? If you do, we're impressed!
- Hold the tool in your hand, and check for rough, sharp, or protruding edges. Make sure the components are easy to open and close.
- Compare the weights of various multitools. They can get quite heavy if they're loaded with features, and while that's great for the versatile outdoorsperson, it's not so great for day-to-day use or even light backpacking. If it's too heavy, you'll leave it at home.
- Check the *torque,* or twisting action. You want a tool that feels solid and strong when sawing or working with screws.
- Safety locks are a must. (Some inexpensive models don't have them.)
- Look for stainless steel with a high carbon content as opposed to iron content. It's less prone to rust. Titanium is another high-quality, durable option, but it's pricey.
- Examine the sharpness of the knife blades. A dull blade can cause more accidents because it requires more force.
- Think twice about getting a tool with extra attachments, like screwdriver bits. They're tiny and easy to lose.

SHOPPING BAGS VERDICT: Don't skimp too much on your multitool. We found that inexpensive models didn't feel as safe and didn't perform nearly as well as higher-priced models, like Leatherman and Swiss Army.

PAINT

- Check the label for VOCs, which stands for volatile organic compounds. VOCs are chemicals that become gases at room temperature. When inhaled, they can cause headaches and other health problems. Generally, the stronger a paint smells, the more VOCs it's likely to contain. For the safest paints, look for ones labeled low-VOC or VOC-free.

- Oil-based paints contain more chemicals than water-based ones like latex and acrylic, and are best used on wood trim or on the exterior of your home.

- Flat-paint finishes are good at hiding imperfections but they are more difficult to clean. High gloss is best for smooth surfaces, as it highlights imperfections.

- For living rooms or bedrooms, we like the soft glow of eggshell or satin finishes.

- Have kids who like to draw on walls? Go for something with a higher sheen—it'll be easier to clean. That said, some brands do make specialized flat-finish paints that also promise easy cleaning.

- For high-humidity areas like bathrooms and kitchens, go for a semi-gloss.

- Don't scrimp too much. Cheap paint won't go on as easily and won't last as long. So when comparing prices, consider how long you want your paint job to last and if you're into repainting frequently. The average paint should last six years; top-quality paints can last for fifteen.

- We don't think paint chips give you a very accurate picture of what the paint will look like on the wall. Instead, we recommend spending a few bucks on small tester cans before you commit to a few gallons of the stuff. This has saved us both a lot of money and headaches.

BONUS BAG: To prevent your skin from getting as painted as the walls, put a heavy moisturizer on your exposed skin before starting the job. It'll make any splatters much easier to remove.

PAINTBRUSHES AND ROLLERS

- Split ends aren't good for hair, but they are good for paintbrushes! Look for bristles that are split or "flagged" on the ends. They'll hold more paint.
- For water-based paints, use a synthetic brush or roller. Synthetic fibers won't absorb the water in your paint.
- For oil-based paints, use brushes and rollers with natural fibers—they'll spread the paint more evenly. Brushes with China (hog hair) bristles and rollers with lambswool covers are good choices.
- To test the quality of the brush, tap the bristles against the counter or gently fan them out. It shouldn't lose too many bristles.
- Longer bristles will provide a smoother finish on larger surfaces that can't be rolled, like windowsills. Sponge brushes give a less smooth finish, but can be easier to control—especially when tackling hard-to-reach areas like the wall behind your toilet.
- When buying a roller, give it a gentle rub and squeeze. The material should spring back quickly. And make sure you're not left holding any lint. It will end up on the wall.
- Check the pile of the roller. Dense pile will hold more paint, meaning an easier, faster application. But the pile should match the type of paint *and* the surface. Here are two general rules: The glossier the paint finish, the shorter the pile. And the smoother the surface, the shorter the pile.

PAPER TOWELS

- Generic brands may be cheaper, but you'll end up using more of them. In our tests, name brands were stronger and more absorbent and therefore better value for the money.
- Some recycled products are not as strong as those made with virgin fibers. So you could end up using more towels to get the job done.
- We like paper towels that come in half sheets. You reduce waste by using half sheets for small spills.
- Avoid printed towels. The ink can transfer to food.

FAST FACT: On average, Americans do twelve hours less housework each week than we did in the 1960s.

And some cleaning products can make the dyes come off onto your countertop or floor. Talk about counterproductive!

POTS AND PANS

- For a starter kitchen, you should have a frying pan, a small saucepan, a large saucepan, and a roasting pan.
- Stay away from thin cookware. It tends to burn food more easily and doesn't last as long. To check, knock on the bottom. A thin pot will sound very tinny. You can get away with a thinner stockpot if you'll only be boiling water in it.
- Pots made with copper heat up the fastest and are the most expensive kind out there.
- Stainless steel is a good overall option for heat conduction and durability. For added performance, look for a stainless-steel pot with a copper bottom.
- Aluminum is lightweight and a good heat conductor, but it can react with acidic foods and change the flavor. If you're concerned about aluminum leaching into your food, look for cookware that is made of anodized aluminum.
- Cast iron can last forever, and because it's so thick, it cooks food very evenly. But it does require extra care, maintenance, and muscle.
- Nonstick pans are a great option for novice chefs and those who want to lower fat intake. But they're not good for searing.
- The best option? Buy a selection of pots and pans, made of a variety of materials.
- Before you buy that cookware set, analyze what you get in it. Some sets offer too many of the same kind of piece.
- Don't pay full price. Pots and pans frequently go on sale.
- Be sure to check the weight of all the different pieces, especially the frying pan. It should feel sturdy but not too heavy to maneuver. Handles should be spot-welded, not screwed on.
- We don't pay more for pots and pans with glass lids. Once things steam up inside, you can't see anything through the glass anyway!

PLASTIC FOOD CONTAINERS (FOR STORING LEFTOVERS)

In our tests, heavy-duty plastic food containers were much more durable than brands designed for short-term use, like Ziploc Snap 'n Seal or GladWare containers. Though initially cheaper, these disposable containers just don't stand up to the abuse of microwaves and dishwashers as well as heavy-duty brands do. Our tests also found that heavy-duty generic containers stack up well against name brands. (As long as you don't play floor hockey with them as we did, they'll hold up just fine.) We also like brands that have a little tab on the lid for easy opening. And check the label to ensure the product is labeled microwave, freezer, and dishwasher safe. That said, even those containers that say *microwave safe* might become hazardous if overheated. After just four minutes in the microwave with some oil, most of our test containers bubbled and burned. And this melted plastic can end up in your food.

POWER DRILLS

- Cordless drills are more expensive but easier to use.
- The higher the voltage, the more powerful the drill. But more voltage means more weight. Hold the drill above your head to make sure you can handle the weight for longer periods of time. A 12-volt drill is a good all-around choice.
- Look for a drill with variable speeds and a reverse. It will make doing and *undoing* the job easier.
- We like a keyless chuck, which means you don't need a key to open and close the adjustable end that holds the drill bit in place.
- Get a grip! Make sure the drill feels comfortable and well balanced in your hand.
- Because they're designed for use at construction sites, professional tools are more versatile, powerful, and weather resistant than cheaper do-it-yourself brands. We think they're worth the investment.

POWER SAWS

- Looking to start a saw collection? Start with a circular saw and a jigsaw (also known as a saber saw).
- We prefer cords on our saws, as they're more powerful and not as expensive as cordless models. Saws do not need to

be as portable as drills, as generally, you'll be sawing in one location, like a workshop, with power outlets nearby.

- With jigsaws, look for one with a speed square. It clamps onto the wood, making the cutting job easier.
- As with power drills, we like saws with variable speeds.
- Look for a saw with carbide-tipped blades—they cut much better than steel.
- Grip the saw in the store to make sure it feels comfortable. Ensure the knobs used to make adjustments are easy to grasp and move.

ROOM SCENTS

- Room scents only mask foul odors. They don't really freshen air and, in fact, they add chemicals to the air.
- The Environmental Protection Agency says most commercially produced room scents contain chemicals that have been linked to cancer, brain damage, and other serious health problems. They can also dull your sense of smell by weakening the signals traveling from your nose to your brain. Limit your use of aerosol air fresheners, and keep solid air fresheners away from kids and pets. (They can be fatal if eaten.)
- We don't recommend buying chemically laden room scents and air fresheners. Open the window, bake some fresh bread (it smells wonderful!), or use baking soda to get rid of bad odors.
- When it comes to natural air fresheners, read the small print. *Aromatherapy* and *naturally scented* products can also contain synthetic and chemical ingredients.
- *Natural* doesn't mean "safe." Inhaling too much of anything can cause adverse reactions like nausea and headaches.
- In large doses, essential oils and scented candles can also be toxic and cause allergic reactions. (See "Candles" on page 84 for more details.)

SMOKE DETECTORS

- There are two types of battery-operated detectors: photoelectric and ionization. Photoelectric alarms are better at sensing slow-smoldering fires. Ionization alarms are better at picking up fast-burning flames. Dual-detection models combine both.

- In our tests, dual-detection alarms didn't respond as quickly as separate components do. We recommend buying a photoelectric alarm *and* an ionization detector.
- Make sure your smoke detector is approved by the Underwriters Laboratory (UL). This means it has met national safety standards.
- It's better to buy a separate carbon monoxide detector because it works best when mounted in a different place than a smoke detector. CM detectors should be placed four to five feet up the wall, while smoke detectors should go on or near the ceiling.
- When shopping for a smoke detector, don't just buy one. Fire prevention experts say the biggest mistake people make is not buying enough of them. The general rule is one detector per floor, including the basement.
- We like models with hush buttons large enough to push with a broom handle. They're easy to shut off in a false alarm, like when dinner gets slightly charred (a common problem for Kristina).

TIRES

- Consider where you drive. Rainy weather will require a tire that grips the road. All-season tires are sufficient for rain and light snow around a city, but if you drive in more serious winter or mountainous conditions, you should have winter tires.
- Consider how much you drive. Low-end tires will have less traction, and the sidewalls will break down faster, but they may meet your needs if you don't drive much. If you make a lengthy commute every day, you should invest in your tires. You won't have to replace them as often, saving money in the long run.
- Your car manual will tell you what size to buy—and take heed! Buying the wrong size will affect fuel economy and mileage.
- Inquire about warranties, as you may get some benefits by going with certain brands over others. Look for warranties that include free replacement.
- Inquire about buying used tires, as this can be a good way to save money.
- Ask whether the cost of new tires will be prorated according to the condition of your old ones. Most major stores have this policy.

- An average tire should last fifty thousand to sixty thousand miles of regular driving.

TOILET BOWL CLEANERS

- You don't need to spend more on a cleaner designed specifically for toilets. All-purpose household cleaners do just as good a job.
- If you clean your toilet regularly, you don't need to use an abrasive chemical cleaner each time. Products containing hydrochloric acid and phosphoric acid are best used for periodic stain removal.
- For regular cleanings or a "green" cleaning option, you can use vinegar, lemon juice, or baking soda.

FAST FACT: A study at the University of Arizona showed that the average office desk was four hundred times dirtier than the average toilet seat. Researchers counted ten thousand germs per square inch on computer keyboards.

- In our tests, toilet pucks and tank cleaners did not last as many flushes as advertised—2000 Flushes lasted about 400 flushes! We also found these products didn't do a great job of cleaning or disinfecting the bowl, and they were expensive to boot.
- We don't recommend buying brush-cleaner all-in-one combos. They don't work any better, and they're very expensive!

WATER PURIFIERS (DO-IT-YOURSELF SYSTEMS)

- Look for filters that have been certified by the National Sanitation Foundation (NSF).
- If you're going with a faucet-mounted filter, check the size of your faucet, as not all filters will fit. Make sure you can return it if you need to.
- With carafe systems, you pour water into a container and allow it to filter through. These filters need to be replaced twice as often as faucet-mounted systems.
- Don't buy a charcoal filter just because it promises to trap chlorine. You can obtain the same effect by simply letting water sit in an open container, either on the counter or in the fridge.

- You absolutely must change your filter regularly! A dirty filter can become a breeding ground for bacteria and can do more harm than good. We like models with a filter-life indicator. Generally, carafe filters need to be changed every two months, and faucet filters every four.
- In our lab tests, no one filter outperformed the rest, and even tap water met federal standards. But in our taste tests, people preferred the taste of faucet-mounted systems to carafe systems.
- Beware of overblown claims about making tap water safer to drink. Most North American tap water is already deemed safe. Sediment has been filtered out, and bacteria have been killed with chlorine. But if you're concerned, check your municipality to learn more about water safety in your area.

The Checkout Counter

Phew! We have just bought a lot of stuff. Now the bad part—it's time to pay up. Keep a close eye on that register. Pricing inaccuracies are common. One recent study found that 40 percent of consumers experience an inaccuracy once a year. Mistakes happen when an item goes on sale and either the price tag or the cash register hasn't been updated. Pricing discrepancies are most typical during busy shopping times (like weekends and holidays), when price scanners are involved, and at large retail chains and department stores where items often go on sale and prices change frequently. Retailers must honor advertised prices, so keep a watchful eye on that price tag and what you're actually charged at the cash register. But this works both ways—so speak up even when you've been given too much change. You don't want to mess with good shopping karma.

While this book has covered hundreds of commonly purchased items, there is a chance we haven't included the exact item you're looking for. Never fear! In that case, be sure to give the chapter introductions a careful reading, as the tips there are applicable to all manner of items in that category. Also, don't forget to let the Ten Shopping Commandments be your guide through any transaction.

Finally, rest assured—our shopping mission continues. We're in the process of buying, researching, and testing dozens upon dozens of new products. Because we really do plan to shop . . . till we drop!

For Further Information

While this book is largely based on our own research and experience, we have interviewed hundreds of experts in various fields from across North America. In addition, we have consulted numerous organizations and sources, some of which may be helpful to shoppers in search of additional information. We recommend bookmarking the following Web sites:

American Academy of Dermatology, *www.aad.org*
*Includes an A-to-Z guide to common skin conditions and dermatological terms

Better Business Bureau, *www.bbb.org*
*Log on and file a complaint or find a local chapter

Consumer Product Safety Commission, *www.cpsc.gov*
*Consider this site your one-stop shop for product recalls and general product safety information

Cosmetics Cop Paula Begoun's home page, *www.cosmeticscop.com*
*Includes loads of product reviews, a great search engine, and excerpts from her popular publications

Food and Drug Administration, *www.fda.gov*
*Offers answers to your frequently asked questions about cosmetics, food labeling, and much, much more

Juvenile Products Manufacturers Association, *www.jpma.org*
*Features tips on baby product safety and baby-proofing your home. Also includes a listing of all JPMA members and links to their Web sites, where available

National Highway Traffic Safety Administration, *www.nhtsa.dot.gov*
*Look no further for vital vehicle recall and safety information

Acknowledgments

We would like to thank our intrepid assistant and researcher, Rosemary Poole, for leaving no stone unturned. Her tenacity and commitment to the cause are unparalleled. We are also extremely grateful to our editor, Julie Doughty, for giving us a chance, sharing the vision, and making this project an enjoyable collaborative effort. This book would not have been possible without our agent, Kim Goldstein, at Susan Golomb Literary Agency, who worked tirelessly with us to hone our ideas and send us in the right direction.

Thanks to our colleagues at Force Four Entertainment for their partnership and Amy Wallner for her design talent, among other things. To Heather Hawthorn-Doyle, Todd Serotiuk, Catherine Aldana, Simone Wilson, Catherine Atyeo, Jadene Stojak, Kim Hannula, Leah Merrell, Tyronne L'Hirondelle, Brian Beard, Mark Pitkethly, Kathleen Stormont, Joanne Braithwaite, Alison Grantham, and all the others who work on the show, we salute you. To the folks at W Network and Fine Living, thank you for taking a leap with us and for the continued support. (We are especially thankful to Michelle van Beusekom from the former WTN who, way back when, didn't kick us out of her office!)

We would like to express our appreciation to the industry experts in a whole range of fields who have generously given us their time and expertise over the years. Most notably, dermatologist Dr. Jason Rivers, physicist Robin Coope, food scientist Dr. Massimo Marcone, sex educator Sue Johanson, and beauty guru Paula Begoun.

Finally, we would like to thank our families (especially K's hubby, Brad) and friends (Lee "redesign" Steg), not only for their encouragement and cheerleading capabilities, but also for continuing to play guinea pigs and enduring years of product testing and domestic upheaval.

Index

About the Authors

In the midst of their careers as award-winning journalists, Anna Wallner and Kristina Matisic decided to give it all up to pursue their real love: shopping. Many afternoons of shoe shopping and brainstorming later, they came up with the concept for *The Shopping Bags*. They are now the creators, hosts, and executive producers of the TV show *The Shopping Bags,* currently airing on Fine Living in the United States and the W Network in Canada. The show has been on the air for five seasons, receiving multiple nominations. The Bags (yes, it's okay to call them that) also contribute to national magazines and newspapers, appear on radio programs and at trade shows, and run an extensive Web site (www.theshoppingbags.com). They live in Vancouver, British Columbia.